D0400944

SUTTON POCKET HISTORIES

THE COLD WAR

PRISCILLA ROBERTS

SUTTON PUBLISHING

For my parents
The two bravest people I know

First published in the United Kingdom in 2000 by
Sutton Publishing Limited · Phoenix Mill
Thrupp · Stroud · Gloucestershire · GL5 2BU

Copyright © Priscilla Roberts, 2000

All rights reserved. No part of this publication may be
reproduced, stored in a retrieval system, or transmitted, in any
form or by any means, electronic, mechanical, photocopying,
recording or otherwise, without the prior permission of the
publisher and copyright holder.

Priscilla Roberts has asserted the moral right to be identified as
the author of this work.

British Library Cataloguing in Publication Data
A catalogue record for this book is available from the British
Library.

ISBN 0-7509-2437-3

Cover picture: Military Parade on Red Square, Moscow,
1 May 1968 (N. Sitnikov/TASS, courtesy Jonathan Falconer)

Typeset in 11/14 pt Baskerville.
Typesetting and origination by
Sutton Publishing Limited.
Printed and bound in England by
J.H. Haynes & Co. Ltd, Sparkford.

Contents

List of Dates

March 1946	Churchill's Iron Curtain speech
	United States criticizes Soviet behaviour towards
	Iran and Turkey; Soviets withdraw forces from Iran
March 1947	Truman Doctrine speech
	Treaty of Dunkirk between Britain and France
June 1947	Announcement of Marshall Plan
July 1947	Kennan article, 'Sources of Soviet Conduct'
September 1947	Rio Treaty to defend Western Hemisphere
October 1947	Cominform established
February 1948	Communist coup in Czechoslovakia
March 1948	Brussels security pact of five West European powers
April 1948	Organization of American States established
May 1948	Creation of Israel; immediately recognized by
	Soviet Union and United States
June 1948	Berlin blockade begins
April 1949	North Atlantic Treaty signed
May 1949	Berlin blockade ends
August 1949	Soviet Union tests atomic bomb
September 1949	Federal Republic of Germany established
October 1949	Chinese Communist Party, led by Mao Zedong,
	proclaims People's Republic of China on Chinese
	mainland
January 1950	Sino–Soviet Treaty of Alliance and Friendship
	Senator Joseph R. McCarthy makes Wheeling,
	Virginia, speech, beginning of McCarthyism
April 1950	NSC 68 recommends massive American
	rearmament
June 1950	North Korea invades South Korea; United States
	successfully urges United Nations intervention
November 1950	Chinese intervention in Korean War
April 1951	Formation of European Coal and Steel Community
September 1951	Signature of Japanese–American peace treaty and
	security treaty and ANZUS Pact
January 1953	Dwight D. Eisenhower becomes US president
March 1953	Death of Stalin
June 1953	Panmunjom armistice agreement effectively ends

	Korean war; United States concludes security treaty with South Korea
	Workers uprising in East Berlin crushed with Soviet assistance
August 1953	CIA-backed coup overthrows Mohammed Mossadeq's government in Iran and restores Shah Reza Mohammed Pahlavi II to power
September 1953	Nikita Khrushchev becomes general secretary of Soviet Communist Party
December 1953	Eisenhower's 'Atoms for Peace' proposal
March 1954	Successful United States testing of hydrogen bomb
May 1954	Vietminh defeat French army at Dienbienphu; French decide to leave Indochina
June 1954	Successful CIA-backed coup against Guatemalan government
July 1954	Geneva accords end First Indochina War, partitioning Vietnam into North and South
September 1954	Creation of SEATO
December 1954	United States–Taiwan security treaty
January–April 1955	First Quemoy–Matsu [Qinmen–Mazu] Taiwan straits crisis
April 1955	Bandung conference of neutral nations
May 1955	West Germany joins NATO
	Soviet Union establishes Warsaw Pact
June 1955	Creation of Baghdad Pact, later CENTO
July 1955	Eisenhower makes 'Open Skies' proposal at Geneva summit conference
November 1955	Successful Soviet testing of large hydrogen bomb
February 1956	Khrushchev denounces Stalin at Soviet Communist Party's twentieth congress
October 1956	Soviet Union crushes Hungarian uprising
November 1956	Suez crisis
January 1957	Announcement of Eisenhower Doctrine for Middle East
March 1957	Treaty of Rome creates European Economic Community

LIST OF DATES

January 1968	Tet offensive in South Vietnam
March 1968	Johnson announces United States decision to seek peace in Vietnam and withdraw
August 1968	Soviet military intervention in Czechoslovakia; Brezhnev announces Brezhnev Doctrine
January 1969	Richard M. Nixon becomes US president
March 1969	Sino–Soviet border clashes on Ussuri River
July 1969	Nixon announces Nixon Doctrine and begins reduction of American troops in Vietnam
October 1969	Willi Brandt becomes West German chancellor, pursues *Ostpolitik*
November 1969	Strategic Arms Limitation talks begin in Helsinki
August 1970	Brandt and Brezhnev sign Soviet–West German Treaty of Non-Aggression in Moscow
July 1971	Kissinger's secret visit to Beijing
September 1971	Quadripartite Pact on Berlin signed
October 1971	United Nations votes to admit People's Republic of China
December 1971	Indo–Pakistani War leads to independence for Bangladesh
February 1972	Nixon visits China, meets Mao Zedong
May 1972	Nixon–Brezhnev meeting in Moscow, where they sign the ABM Treaty and SALT-I
December 1972	West and East Germany sign Basic Treaty
January 1973	United States, South Vietnam and North Vietnam reach peace accord at Paris
March 1973	United States and PRC agree to open liaison offices in each other's capitals
September 1973	President Salvador Allende of Chile overthrown by military coup
October 1973	Yom Kippur War, and beginning of oil crisis
August 1974	Nixon's resignation due to Watergate scandal; Gerald R. Ford becomes US president
September 1974	Emperor Haile Selassie overthrown in Ethiopia
November 1974	Brezhnev–Ford summit meeting at Vladivostock
April 1975	North Vietnam takes over South Vietnam

LIST OF DATES

August 1975	Signature of Helsinki accords
November 1975	Civil war begins in Angola
September 1976	Death of Mao Zedong
January 1977	Jimmy Carter becomes US president
July 1977	War between Ethiopia and Somalia over Ogaden
January 1979	United States and China re-establish full diplomatic relations
February 1979	Overthrow of Shah of Iran
June 1979	Brezhnev and Carter sign SALT-II Treaty at Vienna summit
July 1979	Sandinistas seize power in Nicaragua
November 1979	Beginning of Iranian hostage crisis
December 1979	Soviet invasion of Afghanistan
January 1980	Announcement of Carter Doctrine to protect Persian Gulf region
August 1980	Beginning of Polish Solidarity movement
January 1981	Ronald Reagan becomes US president; American hostages released
December 1981	Martial law declared in Poland; crackdown on Solidarity
June 1982	Strategic Arms Reduction Talks (START) begin in Geneva
November 1982	Death of Brezhnev; succeeded by Yuri Andropov as Soviet Communist Party general secretary
March 1983	Reagan announces Strategic Defense Initiative ('Star Wars')
October 1983	Military intervention in Grenada
	Bomb attack on Beirut barracks of United States troops
February 1984	Death of Andropov; succeeded by Constantin Chernenko as Soviet Communist Party general secretary
March 1985	Death of Chernenko; succeeded by Mikhail Gorbachev as Soviet Communist Party general secretary
November 1985	Reagan–Gorbachev Geneva summit meeting
October 1986	Reagan–Gorbachev Reykjavik summit meeting

November 1986	Exposure of Iran–Contra scandal
December 1987	Reagan–Gorbachev Washington summit meeting; signature of Intermediate-Range and Shorter-Range Missile Treaty
May–June 1988	Reagan visit to Moscow
January 1989	George Bush becomes US president
February 1989	Soviet troops withdrawn from Afghanistan
June 1989	Solidarity wins Polish parliamentary election
	Student demonstrations in Beijing provoke June 4th repression
August 1989	Non-Communist government assumes power in Poland
September 1989	Hungary reopens borders to West
November 1989	Opening and overthrow of Berlin Wall
December 1989	Non-Communist government assumes power in Czechoslovakia
	Overthrow of Nicolae Ceausescu in Rumania
	Bush–Gorbachev Moscow summit meeting
March 1990	Gorbachev elected president of Soviet Union
August 1990	Iraqi invasion of Kuwait
October 1990	East and West Germany reunified
November 1990	CSCE conference proclaims Cold War's end
January 1991	Persian Gulf War begins
July 1991	Dissolution of Warsaw Pact
	Bush and Gorbachev sign START-I Treaty
August 1991	Military coup against Gorbachev foiled by Boris Yeltsin
	Gorbachev resigns as general secretary
December 1991	Soviet Union disbands to become Commonwealth of Independent States

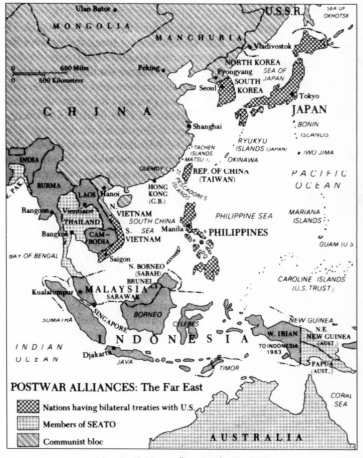

Map 1   Postwar alliances: the Far East
(*From* America: A Narrative History *by George Brown Tindall. Copyright ©
1984 by W.W. Norton & Company, Inc. Used by permission of W.W. Norton
& Company, Inc.*)

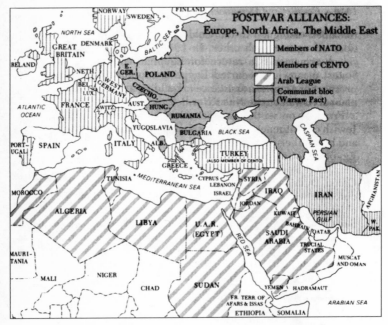

Map 2   Postwar alliances: Europe, North Africa, the Middle East
(*From* America: A Narrative History *by George Brown Tindall. Copyright © 1984
by W.W. Norton & Company, Inc. Used by permission of W.W. Norton &
Company, Inc.*)

Introduction

The term Cold War generally refers to the ideological, geopolitical, and economic international rivalry between the United States and the Soviet Union that characterized the period from approximately 1945 to 1991. These two states, respectively the world's leading capitalist democracy and its most prominent Communist nation, were allies during the Second World War, but within a few years perceived and depicted themselves as locked in desperate competition, a conflict in which each antagonist sought not simply to prevail, but also to win the adherence of as many other countries as possible. The heritage of the Cold War continues to haunt the world today, symbolized by the fact that the current international system has as yet acquired no better descriptive label than 'post-Cold War world order'.

The Cold War began when the successive impact of the First and Second World Wars had destroyed the prevailing international order of the early twentieth century. In 1900 several great European powers, preeminent among them the British empire, Germany, and France, together with Russia and a rising power, Japan, dominated the world. The United States had the economic potential to join this exclusive club but had not yet done so. All the great powers were monarchies and most had extensive colonial possessions, which in many cases they sought to augment. Western empires ruled the Middle East, Africa, and much of Asia. A rough balance of power existed among them.

By 1945 two major wars, conflicts that the American secretary of state Dean Acheson among others characterized as a two-part 'European civil war' in which the interwar years constituted only a truce, had altered this international system beyond recognition or possibility of restoration. The impact of the First World War helped to facilitate the emergence of totalitarian regimes of left and right, officially dedicated to enhancing the lives and self-respect of the general populace even as they imposed authoritarian controls over political, economic, and intellectual matters. In Russia the First World War brought the overthrow in 1917 of Tsar Nicholas I and the creation of the world's first Communist state, the Soviet Union. In Italy in 1923 and Germany in 1933 the war experience and consequent economic and political dislocations contributed substantially to the emergence of Fascist regimes, respectively led by Benito Mussolini and Adolf Hitler, their stated objectives to restore their nations' international standing and win them a place in the sun.

The Second World War, in many respects the result of German and Italian efforts to accomplish these objectives, reduced all European states to the rank of second-class powers, close to bankruptcy and suffering from severe physical war damage, while greatly enhancing the relative standing of both the United States and the Soviet Union. The United States emerged as incomparably the greatest economic power in the world, its industrial plant and superiority decisively enhanced from serving as the 'arsenal of democracy' which provided the *matériel* for the Allied war effort. Although German invasion initially inflicted severe damage on the Soviet Union, Russian economic potential and the sheer size of the Soviet military intimidated its smaller, war-crippled European neighbours. In Asia the war left Japan devastated and defeated and China gravely weakened and wracked by internal revolt and economic difficulties. In most Asian colonies forceful nationalist movements, of varying political complexions, emerged or waxed stronger during the war. These had discredited the European colonial overlords, depriving them of the financial, military, and ideological resources to maintain their grip on their imperial possessions, whose future governmental systems and international alignments generally still remained undetermined.

Historians have disagreed, sometimes bitterly, as to whether considerations of ideology, national security, or economic advantage predominated in causing the Cold War; over which nation, the United States or the Soviet Union, bore the greater responsibility for its development; and on the relative moral merits of the two major protagonists. The Cold War is perhaps best understood as the product of an international power vacuum in both Europe and Asia and of the tensions engendered by the gradual definition, demarcation, and delineation of a new balance of power. Much of the world was in flux as a new system, greatly affected by the developing bipolar Soviet–American antagonism which was both a cause and, increasingly, a self-generating consequence of the Cold War, emerged incrementally. This process took place at varying speeds in different regions, and throughout the Cold War local revisions were nearly always in progress.

In Europe a stable *modus vivendi*, which endured for over four decades, quickly emerged. In much of Asia, Africa, and Latin America, by contrast, the situation was far more fluid, the result of both the fundamental insecurity of numerous existing governments and the degree to which the Second World War weakened the European colonial empires. As Europe stabilized, the Cold War quickly shifted its focus from that continent to other regions, especially Asia and the Middle East. Despite the emergence of a consciously non-aligned group of states, the two great powers tended to perceive all international questions through the prism of their overriding mutual competition for predominance. This tendency led the United States to intervene in two major Asian conflicts, the Korean civil war which began in 1950, and the Vietnamese civil war which, in varying guises, continued throughout the three decades from 1945 to 1975.

One pronounced Cold War feature was the relative caution major powers displayed when dealing with each other. Despite mutual protestations of irreconcilable hostility, in practice the United States and the Soviet Union shared certain common interests, to the extent that one historian has termed the period 'the long peace'. Although in Korea and Vietnam alike both the

United States and the Soviet Union assisted opposing parties involved in direct hostilities, in neither conflict did either great power ever seriously consider any outright declaration of war against the other. Indeed, in both struggles restricting their intervention so as to preclude such an outcome was a prominent, if tacit, preoccupation of both major powers. The successive development of atomic and thermonuclear weapons enabled each big power to inflict near devastation upon its rival, but only at the cost of its own destruction. Consequently, from the mid-1950s onwards the two antagonists launched efforts to reach some understanding on the use of such weapons. The Cuban missile crisis of 1962, the occasion when a nuclear exchange seemed most likely, had a sobering effect on both big powers and, indeed, on the rest of the world.

Concurrently, the international scene became more complicated, challenging attempts at bipolar definitions. As defence budgets soared and innovative technology grew ever more expensive, attempts to reduce military spending appeared increasingly attractive. In 1949 the emergence of a Communist regime in China, a country with one-quarter of the world's population, appeared a major victory for the Soviet camp, one likely to advance the Communist cause throughout Asia. Yet by the late 1950s growing hostility between China and the Soviet Union effectively divided the two major Communist powers, a situation which smaller socialist countries, such as Vietnam, could often manipulate to their own advantage. In the late 1960s and early 1970s the United

States successfully exploited the intra-Communist split, symbolized by bloody Sino–Soviet border clashes in 1969, to move towards détente with both the Soviet Union and the People's Republic of China, whose government American leaders had previously refused to recognize. The results included several nuclear arms limitation agreements, the relaxation of East–West tensions in Europe, and a *de facto*, albeit limited, Sino–American alignment.

From the later 1970s until the mid-1980s, a period one historian has termed the 'second Cold War', Soviet–American tensions again accelerated. In 1980 the election in the United States of a conservative president, Ronald Reagan, who vowed to combat what he characterized as the Soviet 'evil empire', seemed to herald a further hardening of Cold War positions, symbolized by his endorsement of high defence budgets and the 'Star Wars' anti-missile system. Yet the Soviet selection in 1985 of a moderate and innovative Communist Party secretary, Mikhail Gorbachev, and growing Russian economic problems, rapidly changed the very nature of the Cold War. Within two years the two superpowers reached the first of several agreements to reduce nuclear weapons, and in 1989 Gorbachev withdrew Soviet troops from Afghanistan. That same year the Warsaw Pact collapsed as he permitted non-Communist governments to assume power in the Soviet satellites in Eastern Europe. In October 1990 the two Germanies were reunited, and the next month the Conference on Security and Cooperation in Europe declared the end of the Cold War. A year later, in December 1991, the Soviet Union itself dissolved, to become the short-lived Commonwealth of Independent States.

As John Lewis Gaddis pointed out in *We Now Know* (1997), until the 1990s a Cold War historian inescapably wrote from the perspective of one living in the era under discussion, a viewpoint which tended – and the pervasive memories of which sometimes still tend – to make detached analysis somewhat difficult to attain. Moreover, until Soviet, Eastern European, and even some Chinese archives began to open in the 1990s, historians enjoyed access – and even that partial – only to Western sources on the Cold War, making any discussion of the preoccupations, mindset, motivation, and policies of Communist bloc countries and leaders largely speculative. Even now, much material from both sides of the divide remains closed, and a definitive history of the Cold War will not appear for decades, if ever. Yet, such caveats notwithstanding, in the year 2000 we can at least begin to escape from the often overly simplistic and even propagandist analyses which marred much writing on the Cold War and look back at the period Richard Crockatt has termed the 'fifty years' war' with a new understanding of the complexities and ambiguities which almost certainly characterized its emergence, development and impact.

ONE

The European Dimension, 1945–1950

Historians have argued over almost every aspect of the Cold War, including the precise date it began. Some trace its origins as early as 1918, shortly after Bolshevik revolutionaries led by Vladimir Ilyich Lenin established a Communist government in Russia. The United States joined Britain, France, and Japan in sending troops to Siberia, forces whose stated objective was merely to keep the trans-Siberian railway line open and protect Allied supplies near Vladivostock against German seizure. In practice America's partners quickly expanded this undertaking, which lasted until spring 1920, into attempts to overthrow Communist rule in Russia. Until 1933 the United States, unlike other Western powers, refused to recognize the Soviet government. Even after recognition Soviet–American relations remained cool throughout the 1930s, though despite the purges which the dictatorial Soviet leader Josef Stalin initiated, many leftist Western intellectuals and romantic idealists believed Soviet Communism offered a political model superior to that enjoyed by their own countries. Most Americans, by contrast, feared and deplored Soviet Communism, considering it the complete antithesis of the American free enterprise system, destructive of those individual rights to 'life, liberty, and the pursuit of happiness' enshrined in the Declaration of Independence, and irreligious to boot.

Despite pronounced Soviet–American ideological antagonism and predominantly cool relations between the two powers, it took a major war to bring their interests into outright collision. During the 1930s the bellicose behaviour and territorial demands of increasingly restive Germany and Italy led Western powers and the Soviet Union to adopt different strategies for dealing with the Fascist powers. Great Britain, France, and even the United States initially acquiesced in the expansionist policies of the German Führer, Adolf Hitler, symbolized by the September 1938 Munich agreement, which ceded much of Czechoslovakia to Germany. This gave way in 1939 to a determination to rearm and make no further concessions. Stalin, by contrast, was apprehensive that, should the German Reich attack Soviet territory, Western powers would leave Russia to face Fascist Germany unassisted. In August 1939 he concluded a Non-Aggression Pact with Hitler, which safeguarded the Eastern German frontier against Soviet attack. In a compact recalling the eighteenth-century partitions of Poland, the two signatories also agreed to collaborate in invading that state, whose territory separated them, and dividing it between themselves. The Non-Aggression Pact effectively freed Germany to begin the Second World War, counting the Soviet Union, supposedly a sworn ideological opponent, as a friendly neutral or even a tacit confederate, which until 1941 provided Germany with substantial amounts of war supplies.

The wartime alliance between the United States, Britain, and the Soviet Union was based decidedly on convenience, not mutual trust. In June 1941 Hitler, having subdued most of Western Europe, including France, the Low Countries, and Scandinavia, in the blitzkrieg launched in spring 1940, chose to invade the Soviet Union. Following the time-hallowed principle that the enemy of my enemy is my friend, Britain and the United States, by this time virtual *de facto* allies against Hitler even though the Americans had yet to declare war, immediately embraced Stalin as a fellow victim of Hitler. Winston Churchill, the dogged British wartime prime minister, characteristically remarked: 'If Hitler invaded Hell he would at least make a favourable reference to the Devil!' Russia immediately joined the beneficiaries of the new Lend-Lease programme, under which the United States was already sending war supplies in bulk to other opponents of Hitler and Japan. After the Pearl Harbor attack of December 1941, when both Germany and Japan declared war on the United States, the 'big three' powers were formally allied against Hitler.

Serious strains afflicted their relationship. Although official propaganda portrayed the three allies as sharing common objectives, sedulously glossing over the substantial ideological and practical differences separating their political systems, within each country many officials remained decidedly wary of their supposed confrères. Until 1945 Stalin regularly suspected that Britain and France might make a separate peace, abandoning him to face the might of Hitler unassisted. Churchill and Franklin D. Roosevelt, the wartime American president, were similarly apprehensive that the Soviet Union might individually negotiate peace with Germany. In the Atlantic Charter both signed in August 1941, Churchill and Roosevelt committed their countries to war aims which included the famous 'Four Freedoms', the rights of nations to self-determination and to internal political, economic, and religious freedom, but Stalin declined their invitations to endorse these objectives. Initially Stalin hoped his Anglo–American allies would open a second front in France in 1942, thus relieving the pressure on the Soviet forces and populace who faced the German military unaided. The decision to defer this invasion, first to 1943 and then to 1944, caused him to believe with some justification that his allies had chosen to expend Russian lives to win the war. Soviet wartime losses amounted to at least 20 million dead, as well as enormous devastation to property and industrial plant, since over the three years 1941 to 1944 the Soviet war zone absorbed at least three-quarters of the effort of the German military machine.

Anglo–American strategic decisions to postpone the West European invasion to June 1944 carried important implications for postwar Europe. At the Teheran conference, held in late 1943, the Allied leaders decided that

Soviet troops would be left to defeat the German occupying forces – or in Rumania and Hungary, allied forces which controlled most East European countries, including Poland, Hungary, Czechoslovakia, Rumania, Bulgaria, and Albania, states which by early 1945 were under *de facto* Soviet control. As Soviet military conquest reached into Eastern Germany, Stalin considered the extension of Soviet power to Eastern Europe a matter of Soviet national security. Twice since 1900, in 1914 and 1941, Germany had invaded Russia, and between the wars most East European and Balkan states were anti-Soviet in orientation, allied with either France or Germany. By ensuring Soviet dominance of Eastern Europe and the Balkans and keeping postwar Germany permanently weak, Stalin was determined to prevent the recurrence of this scenario, plans he had some reason to believe his allies would effectively tolerate.

On occasion in 1943 and 1944 Churchill conveyed to Roosevelt and other Americans his apprehensions that when the war ended an undependable Soviet Communist regime, quite possibly hostile to the Western powers, would dominate much of Eastern Europe, but Roosevelt generally minimized his fears, leaving him little alternative but pragmatically to acquiesce in informal understandings demarcating Soviet and British power in the Balkans. The unofficial 'percentages agreement' which Roosevelt and Stalin reached in 1944 placed Greece within the British sphere of influence, Rumania and Bulgaria within the Soviet, and acknowledged both British and Soviet interests in Hungary and Yugoslavia.

Germany and Poland, the traditional invasion pathway from Germany into Russia, were more problematic. Stalin uncompromisingly intended to retain the Eastern Polish territory he had seized in 1939, compensating Poland by transferring to her formerly German lands east of the Oder–Neisse line, and to control Poland through the Soviet-dominated puppet Lublin government which he installed in January 1945. Moreover, brooking no opposition to Russian dominance, he attempted to eliminate potential anti-Soviet leaders. As early as 1939 Russian soldiers massacred many thousands of captured Polish officers at Katyn and elsewhere. When Polish resistance fighters launched an autumn 1944 Warsaw uprising, assuming that approaching Soviet forces would quickly assist them, Stalin allowed the Germans to destroy the Polish opposition before deploying Russian troops to mop up the surviving Germans. At the Yalta conference of February 1945 Stalin effectively won British and American acquiescence in his control of Eastern Europe, but he made a promise to hold 'free and unfettered elections' in Poland and other states. Within two weeks the Soviets imposed a subservient government upon Rumania, evidence of how little weight their pledges carried, although until 1948 Stalin continued to tolerate elected governments with substantial non-Communist elements in Czechoslovakia and Hungary.

The Allies had little real leverage over Soviet behaviour in Eastern Europe, an area whose control Stalin considered vital to Soviet security and therefore would not compromise. There is some reason to suppose that Stalin believed that he and his Western allies, effectively dividing Europe into spheres of influence, had left defeated Italy and liberated France under Anglo–American dominance, free from Soviet interference. In early 1945, moreover, Roosevelt eagerly sought Soviet support for the United Nations and Soviet entry into the continuing war against Japan which, until atomic bombs were successfully tested in July 1945, was expected to last at least until 1946.

To avoid precipitating inter-allied tensions, throughout the war, even as late as the last summit conferences, the final settlement of many issues, including the postwar government of Germany, was deferred until a later date. Since 1940, however, the Western allies had committed themselves in principle to the self-determination of peoples, views which informed the United Nations Organization whose creation the Big Three wartime allies endorsed at the spring 1945 San Francisco conference. By early 1945 wartime propaganda emphasizing the supposed commitment of the Big Three powers to identical war aims and ideals was wearing thin, and the defeat of Germany eliminated the once overriding concern to paper over all such divisions to facilitate the battle against a common enemy. Ideological and stylistic differences among the former allies, as well as their divergent war aims, assumed new significance.

It soon became apparent that Soviet and Western interests in Europe would not be easily reconciled. Stalin's pronouncedly paranoid and suspicious personality may have been largely responsible, as Gaddis has suggested in *We Now Know* (1997). It virtually precluded him from trusting or reaching lasting agreements with either his allies or the Soviet satellites in Eastern Europe, which made the Cold War close to inevitable. Yet while Stalin's temperamental peculiarities undoubtedly exacerbated the inability of the former allies to negotiate the compromises necessary to solid agreements during the Cold War, developing strains and tensions among them also reflected very real divisions and dramatically different priorities. The prevailing power vacuum in Europe exacerbated Soviet–Western frictions, as did the absence of real communication or understanding between Soviets and Westerners. Europeans and Americans enjoyed a wide range of official and personal contacts with each other, running the gamut from personal friendships and intermarriages, through shared educational, business, and governmental ties. Whatever their disagreements, elites on both sides of the Atlantic could readily comprehend the preoccupations, priorities, and ways of doing business of their counterparts. Under Communism Soviet officials were precluded from developing such links with their Western opposite numbers; indeed overmuch official, let alone personal, contact with Westerners might well bring disgrace, banishment, even death. Ideological hostility compounded this mutual incomprehension, facilitating rapid postwar deterioration in Soviet–Western relations.

As war ended in Europe, German and Italian power lay in ruins. France, defeated in 1940 and partially occupied by Germany until late 1944, lacked the economic and moral resources to replace them. Britain, one of the Big Three allied powers, emerged from the war victorious but effectively dependent upon the United States economically, and, with the abrupt end of Lend-Lease, desperately seeking a substantial loan to facilitate recovery. Despite American aid, war costs forced Britain to liquidate most of its over-seas investments and foreign exchange holdings and incur huge new debts, making any major independent overseas role impossible. Though technologically backward, the Soviet army was by far the largest military force in Europe, an intimidating colossus even after its numbers fell from 11.9 million in 1945 to somewhere between 2.9 million and 4 million three years later. Soviet military dominance now extended from the Pacific to the Elbe; the Baltic states, Latvia, Estonia, and Lithuania, were incorporated in the Soviet Union in 1940; and Finland, though formally independent, only remained so on Soviet sufferance. The violence and brutality with which Soviet officials imposed their rule upon Eastern Europe, allowing troops to loot and rape at will, dispossessing many Poles and Germans, and summarily disposing of political opponents, made Russian domination appear even less attractive. For West European nations, the United States represented the only available potential counterbalance against a menacing Russian neighbour whose forces, whether or not their intentions were peaceable, were uncomfortably close. Excluding whatever reparations they might extract from their defeated enemies, North America was also the only available substantial source of outside economic aid to finance their recovery from the ravages of war.

The United States was the only power to end the Second World War with its international position both economically and strategically enhanced. Its gross national product rose from $88.6 billion in 1939 to $220 billion ($135 billion in constant dollars) in 1945, as American industrial production furnished the bulk of the *matériel* for the joint allied war effort. Productive plant and industrial output grew by over 50 per cent, and half the manufacturing in the world took place in the United States. Washington possessed almost two-thirds of the total gold reserves and half the shipping in the world; as the greatest international exporter, even several years later it supplied one-third of all global exports. When the war ended the American army numbered 12.5 million and three years later was still 1.3 million. Its fleet was the largest in the world, with 1,200 major warships, and its air force of over 3,000 heavy and ultra-long-range bombers second to none. Although Britain had shared in development, the United States also had a monopoly of the atomic bomb.

Some Americans and many Europeans feared a repetition of the post-1918 scenario, when the United States declined to enter the new League of Nations and, while not eschewing all international involvement, followed fundamentally unilateralist policies. By 1945, however, this seemed unlikely. Within and outside the United States government there existed a group of officials, many temporarily seconded from the world of international finance and law, deeply committed to what was in some cases a near religious faith that their country should be far more active in world affairs. In many cases such men, among the most prominent of them Henry L. Stimson, secretary of state under Herbert Hoover and secretary of war from 1940 to 1945, consciously felt themselves heirs to an internationalist tradition stretching back to the muscular diplomacy of President Theodore Roosevelt in the early 1900s. Franklin Roosevelt himself essentially shared these assumptions. Believing that international economic barriers and structural imbalances had largely contributed to the Great Depression and the consequent emergence of irredentist authoritarian states during the 1930s, such officials strongly advocated the creation of a liberal world economic order based on free trade and convertible currencies. At the Bretton Woods conference of 1944 the United States was instrumental in establishing the International Monetary Fund and the International Bank for Reconstruction and Development, institutions designed to finance postwar recovery. United States support was also crucial to the creation in 1945 of the United Nations, an organization effectively dominated by the great powers, its mission primarily to settle international conflicts without resort to war and to do so more successfully than its predecessor, the League of Nations.

This heavy reliance on international organizations betokened the distinctly limited nature of the expanded foreign obligations which Roosevelt and many other American officials initially supported. From 1943 onwards Roosevelt envisaged a postwar world in which each of the great powers or 'Four Policemen', the United States, Britain, China, and the Soviet Union, would have a sphere of influence – respectively Latin America, the

British empire and Western Europe, Asia, and Eastern Europe – within which maintaining order would be primarily its own responsibility. After 1945, therefore, the United States rapidly reduced its military forces, particularly the European and Asian contingents. While as early as 1943 there had been some influential United States military men and civilian officials who believed that their national security required the acquisition of a network of bases around the world and the development of a large standing military, with the industrial infra- structure to support a major war effort, and while some, like James V. Forrestal, secretary of the navy and later the first American secretary of defense, also viewed the Soviet Union as potentially the future enemy, in general American officials hoped that their overseas commit- ments would be modest and that future international organizations would bear the primary responsibility of providing both military security and economic relief. Between 1945 and 1950 the United States was to expand its international role dramatically, but the process was slow and incremental.

As the Second World War ended, Soviet–Western relations rapidly degenerated. Although the Western powers made no serious attempt to challenge Soviet domination over Eastern Europe, the harshness with which Stalin imposed Russian rule contributed to a broad Western distaste for the Soviets. The sudden death in April 1945 of Franklin D. Roosevelt, and his replace- ment by the less diplomatic Harry S. Truman, who – to the latter's intense chagrin – soon sternly lectured V.I.

Molotov, the Soviet foreign minister, on the Russian failure to honour the Yalta provisions for free East European elections, rather chilled relations. In May 1945 the United States abruptly ended Lend-Lease aid, while floating suggestions to the Soviet Union that modifications of Soviet behaviour in Eastern Europe would win them a substantial American loan.

Perhaps most importantly, the American failure in August 1945 to inform Stalin of the destructive capacity of its atomic weapons before two were detonated over the Japanese cities of Hiroshima and Nagasaki intensified growing Soviet distrust of Western intentions. Despite heated historiographical debate on the question, it seems unlikely that their desire to intimidate the Soviet Union was the major reason impelling the Western allies to use atomic weapons against Japan, where military extremists still retained substantial power and, despite the urban devastation wreaked by ferocious allied bombing, opposed surrender. Even so, the successful testing of a nuclear device during the Potsdam conference of July 1945 undoubtedly inclined American and British leaders to be less conciliatory towards Stalin. The Soviet dictator, disregarding the pressing need to repair serious war damage, certainly perceived nuclear weapons as potentially threatening to his country and immediately instituted a major crash programme to develop a Russian bomb.

American efforts in 1946 to dedicate atomic energy to peaceful uses and to bring it under international control foundered on Soviet reluctance to abandon its own nuclear programme or subject it to inspection while leaving the United States with a virtual nuclear monopoly, in exchange for vague promises to destroy such weapons at some unspecified future date. The United States found Soviet counterproposals equally unsatisfactory. The discovery in early 1946 that a Soviet spy ring had successfully transmitted atomic secrets to Moscow further exacerbated the issue.

Well before these schemes foundered, Soviet–American relations deteriorated dramatically. The Allies had never reached any firm agreement on the postwar treatment of Germany. At the 1943 Teheran conference it was agreed that Soviet and Western forces would invade Germany from the East and West respectively; that the Russians would take Berlin, the German capital; and that each nation would occupy part of Germany, which would ultimately be united under a government acceptable to all the occupying powers. Initially, some American officials advocated more punitive measures. In 1944 American Treasury representatives, fearing future German resurgence, advanced plans to weaken Germany permanently by dividing it into several states and destroying most of its industrial capacity. The War Department opposed such extreme measures, since the German economy was the engine which would drive the postwar recovery of other European states, making Europe once more self-sufficient and independent of American aid. In spring 1945, as German defeat loomed, Roosevelt rejected passionate pleas from Churchill that the Allies should break their wartime agreements on

14

Germany and dispatch American troops to take and withhold from Soviet control as much German territory as possible, including Berlin.

To compensate for their own wartime deprivations the Soviets were determined to extract heavy reparations from Germany, whatever the impact on their defeated enemy, whereas the United States, anxious to facilitate German reintegration into Europe and mindful of the lengthy difficulties which Allied demands for German reparations precipitated after the First World War, opposed their imposition. At the Potsdam conference, where the Allied leaders agreed to treat Germany as one economic entity, the harshness with which Soviet troops extorted compensation from their East German occupation sector, stripping everything valuable, shocked the assembled British and American officials. Initially the United States and Britain shipped reparations in kind from their zones to the Soviets, but suspecting that they were utilizing the reparations programme to cripple the German economy permanently, and reluctant to provide humanitarian aid to their own German sectors which the Soviets would effectively funnel off, in May 1946 they ceased such payments.

This decision coincided with growing tensions in Soviet–Western relations over Iran, in the Middle East. Wherever possible, it seems, the Soviets sought to maximize their international advantages. During the war Soviet and British troops occupied Iran to safeguard its rich oil holdings from German takeover. At Yalta the Soviets unsuccessfully sought major Iranian oil concessions in exchange for withdrawing their troops, which remained in place until 1946. In January that year renewed intimidating Soviet demands for such concessions, together with aggressive suggestions that Turkey allow Soviet warships unrestricted passage through the Dardanelles straits, the strategically vital outlet from the Black Sea to the Mediterranean, created new alarms. The United States responded forcefully by stating its strong backing of Iran, demanding the withdrawal of Soviet troops, and sending its most powerful warship to Turkish waters, whereupon the Soviets yielded on all points.

Despite the relative Russian caution demonstrated in these episodes, Western officials focused on what they viewed as the expansionist character of Soviet foreign policy. American and British policymakers bore very much in mind what they perceived as the 'lessons' of the 1930s, especially the Munich crisis of 1938, that yielding to dictators merely whetted their appetite for more, ultimately making war inevitable, whereas initial firm and determined resistance would normally cause an international aggressor to back down. Increasingly, Western officials perceived the Soviet Union in terms of 'red fascism', an authoritarian state resembling in all but its official ideology their defeated Second World War opponents, Germany and Italy. Stalin stoked such fears when, on 9 February 1946, he publicly characterized the next Russian five-year economic plan as necessary preparation for inevitable conflict with the capitalist powers.

At this point the Truman administration requested George F. Kennan, counsellor in the United States embassy in Moscow and a Soviet expert, to explain the rationale behind Russian policies. In perhaps the seminal document of the Cold War, Kennan replied with an 8,000-word telegram. It stated that, since Soviet antagonism towards the West arose from the need of Russian rulers to justify their oppressive domestic rule as essential to combat the hostility of foreign powers, Western states could do little to alter Soviet policies. Instead, they must adopt policies of 'containment', firmly resisting attempts to expand Soviet influence while awaiting internal changes which would alter the nature of Soviet government. Kennan's telegram, circulated throughout the higher echelons of American government, and his subsequent article 'The Sources of Soviet Conduct', published in the influential quarterly *Foreign Affairs*, quickly became definitive documents of United States Cold War strategy. Kennan returned to Washington to head the newly created Policy Planning Staff, charged with the long-range planning and conceptualization of United States foreign policy. Until the early 1990s the word 'containment' would fundamentally describe American policies toward the Soviet Union.

British and European leaders had good reasons to encourage American involvement; indeed, the historian Geir Lundestad has characterized United States dominance of Western Europe as an 'empire by invitation'. Aware that even united they could not match Soviet military strength, and fearful that internal economic weakness might make their nations easy prey to both internal Communist subversion and external threat,

Western leaders actively sought to persuade the United States to assume far greater European responsibilities than ever before. The British, until the Second World War still the world's greatest power, took the lead in this effort. Britain, no longer a superpower, and now outmatched by both the United States and the Soviet Union, while determined to maintain its great power status, was too weak to do so without American support and acquiescence; and throughout the Cold War generally acted as a loyal lieutenant to the United States, while continuing to shoulder disproportionately large overseas defence and other commitments. This enabled Britain to 'punch above its weight' on the international scene, but the emphasis on military spending and Britain's world role may also have led the British economy to lag behind those of other West European countries.

In the crucial early Cold War years British officials encouraged and exhorted their American counterparts to embark upon new economic and military commitments in Europe and then to enlarge them. Most dramatically, in March 1946 the towering figure of Churchill, the legendary British wartime prime minister who, now out of office, had all the prestige of 'the greatest living Englishman', spoke out at Fulton, Missouri. An 'iron curtain', he said, had descended over Europe, with freedom on one side, totalitarian despotism on the other. British and Americans must unite to oppose its further extension. Stalin and some Americans strongly criticized Churchill's speech, which was cleared in advance with the Truman administration and endorsed by the new British Labour government. Other European pleas soon followed.

In February 1947 British officials informed the American government that economic difficulties prevented them continuing their aid to Greece and Turkey, countries bordering the strategically important supply routes for Middle Eastern oil. In 1946/47 Europe suffered its hardest winter for many years, closing factories and generating severe food and fuel shortages, rising inflation, and social unrest. Europe also faced an annual balance of payments deficit surpassing $5 billion. Severe strikes in France and the growing electoral strength of both French and Italian Communist parties raised the possibility that two major West European nations would move into the Communist camp, shifting the European balance of forces immensely in Soviet favour. The British government took the lead in aggressively seeking American assistance in all these assorted problems.

In March President Truman not only publicly supported an extensive aid programme for Greece and Turkey, but presented this in the context of an American commitment to assist any country where democracy was threatened either externally or internally. The effectively unlimited global pledge of the 'Truman Doctrine' paved the way for secretary of state George C. Marshall to announce a major economic aid programme for all European nations. The Soviet Union and its satellites soon boycotted the European Recovery Plan, usually termed the Marshall Plan, while non-Communist nations participated in a coordinated four-year enterprise to enhance their economic performance and make the European economies once more self-sustaining.

Historians have debated the precise impact of American aid, with some suggesting that it had little impact on already improving European economies, and others arguing that it made the crucial difference between success and stagnation. There can be little doubt, however, that the Plan made a substantial contribution. Its final report, in 1952, noted that overall West European industrial production had increased by 64 per cent since 1947 and 41 per cent over prewar levels; from 1947 to 1952 coal, aluminium, copper, and cement production levels grew by 27 per cent, 69 per cent, 31 per cent, and 90 per cent respectively. European populations were able to resume a normal way of life and regain self-confidence. The Plan also set a precedent for continued European cooperation, facilitating the creation in 1950 of the European Coal and Steel Community, the precursor of today's European Union.

Yet the Plan further divided Western from Eastern Europe and intensified the Cold War. Essential to successful Western European recovery was German economic revival, at least in those sectors under American, British, and French occupation. It seems that one major Soviet preoccupation was to keep Germany weak, unable to start a third European war or invade Russia again. Soviet security concerns were incompatible, therefore, with the Western European quest for economic recovery, and Soviet–Western relations were so poor as to render any understanding or negotiated compromise unattainable. Two Russian historians, Vladislav Zubok and Constantine Pleshakov, even suggest that for the Soviets the Marshall Plan marked the real beginning of the Cold War. They responded by tightening control over Eastern Europe. In October 1947 Stalin also announced the establishment of the Cominform, a trans-European grouping of nine major Communist parties, whom he expected to sabotage the Marshall Plan, and in 1948 Communist coups overthrew democratically elected governments in Hungary and Czechoslovakia.

Most flamboyantly, in June 1948, after currency reforms were introduced in the now merged Western occupation sectors of Germany, the Soviet Union responded by cutting off land access to western Berlin, the symbolically significant former German capital, deep in the Soviet sector, where each of the three Western occupying powers, Britain, France, and the United States, had been assigned zones which were later merged into one. Soviet obduracy met American resolve; for eleven months a massive airlift ferried all essential supplies into West Berlin, while a Western counterblockade of the Soviet zone proved economically damaging. Demonstrating the practical caution which often characterized Cold War crises, the Western powers avoided any potential direct military confrontation with Soviet forces by eschewing attempts to resupply Berlin by road across Soviet-occupied territory.

The Berlin blockade contributed to the Western decision to abandon hope of German reunification and establish a separate state, the Federal Republic of Germany, in the former Western occupation sectors. With its foundation in 1949, the territorial borders of Cold War Europe were clearly delineated. The first Berlin crisis also persuaded the United States to conclude a permanent military alliance with most West European states, finally jettisoning the warnings of George Washington, its first president, against any such commitments. Initially, the Truman administration had sought to limit American involvement in Europe to economic aid, hoping that Britain would bear the primary responsibility for European continental defence, and in 1947 Britain and France had signed the Dunkirk Treaty, a mutual defence pact, expanded the following year to become the Brussels Pact, which brought Belgium, the Netherlands, and Luxembourg under its umbrella. Ernest Bevin, the British foreign minister, repeatedly urged the United States that, without its participation, such arrangements would fail to reassure Western European states that they were secure against Russian attack, which in turn would undercut the economic achievements of the Marshall Plan. The Berlin blockade gave such pleas added force.

In 1949 the United States, Canada, and fourteen European countries concluded the North Atlantic Treaty. Under its terms an attack on one signatory would automatically be considered an assault on all, including the nuclear-armed United States, a deterrent so effective that there was never to be such an assault. West Germany was not a founding NATO member, although NATO troops were stationed on German soil, some suggested to assure nervous NATO allies of compliant future German behaviour. The wealth and sizeable population of Germany represented military assets too appreciable to be permanently excluded, and in 1955 the German Federal Republic joined the alliance, prompting the Soviet Union in turn to establish the Warsaw Pact, a similar military grouping of its East European satellites.

By 1950 the European situation was essentially stable, with clearly defined boundaries demarcating Western and Soviet spheres of influence. Throughout the Cold War, their respective European alliances and associated security interests remained the primary foci of both Soviet and United States policy. Rhetorical flights on both sides notwithstanding, in practice each respected the interests of its rival, understanding that their opponent considered these areas vital to its own security and would respond strongly to any encroachments. Successive crises in Eastern Europe – the Berlin uprising in 1953, the Hungarian and Czech crises of 1956 and 1968, and the repression of the Polish Solidarity movement in 1981 – failed to win any but moral support from the West. Elsewhere in the world, by contrast, the situation was more fluid, providing opportunities for either the Communist or capitalist camps to gain at the expense of the other. From 1950 onwards, therefore, the focus of the Cold War shifted from Europe towards international regions more fundamentally peripheral to its original emphasis.

TWO

Korea to Vietnam, 1950–1975

The extension of the Cold War beyond Europe occurred in the context of a changing international order. The weakening of European colonial empires consequent on the Second World War left much of Asia in a state of flux, the nature of its future governments unclear. Whereas Japan experienced American occupation for several years, in 1949 a lengthy civil war brought a Communist government to power in China. In the Middle East, the diminution of British power offered the United States valuable political and economic opportunities, while Israel, a small, vulnerable new state, quickly became an American client. In Latin America, the United States' own backyard, authoritarian governments frequently faced radical threats. As African states decolonized, their allegiances likewise became targets for Soviet–American competition. Surprisingly quickly the United States amassed a global network of allies, clients, pacts, and commitments which, while none was formally a colony, effectively constituted an empire. The Soviet Union, though more cautious in assuming binding military commitments, offered its own aid programmes to potentially sympathetic governments and military assistance to revolutionary movements around the world.

By 1949 the European Cold War was rapidly stabilizing, as the Marshall Plan took effect and NATO was established. At least some American government officials nonetheless felt a pervasive sense of threat, due in part to Russia's successful detonation of an atomic bomb in August 1949 and the seizure of power by the Chinese Communist Party in October. In January 1950 President Truman authorized the development of a hydrogen bomb, substantially more powerful and destructive than the first atomic bombs. Various officials in the State and Defense departments, led by Paul H. Nitze, who had replaced Kennan as head of the Policy Planning Staff, argued that should war break out, the United States lacked the military resources to meet even its existing international commitments. Implicitly, they endorsed the 1947 'Truman Doctrine' for American assistance to any nation facing internal or external Communist threat.

A planning paper NSC 68, which they drafted and eventually delivered to Truman in April 1950, demanded massive enhancements in American conventional and nuclear military capabilities, including substantially increased American troop contributions to NATO forces in Europe, stating: 'Without superior aggregate military strength, in being and readily mobilisable, a policy of "containment" . . . is no more than a policy of bluff.' NSC 68 envisaged increasing the existing United States defence budget from $13.5 billion to anywhere between $18 and $50 billion, recommendations the economy-conscious Truman initially rejected, although ultimately he might have endorsed more modest increases.

By 1949 American officials, with Truman's enthusiastic encouragement, had begun to perceive postcolonial nations around the world as potential recruits to the camps of either Communism or liberal capitalist democracy. The Point Four programme Truman announced in his 1949 inaugural address promised technological assistance to developing countries. American policymakers, convinced that poverty and maldistribution of wealth greatly enhanced the appeal of Communism, believed that United States aid could counteract this. In 1961 President John F. Kennedy was to establish another agency, the Peace Corps, to channel the idealism of youthful Americans into constructive efforts to aid developing countries in Africa, Asia, and Latin America. Two years later 7,000 Peace Corps volunteers were assigned to forty-four countries, working on largely unglamorous but productive enterprises. By 1985 the Corps had recruited over 100,000 volunteers. Unlike many such agencies, the Peace Corps sedulously attempted to avoid becoming a front for American intelligence operations, and deployed volunteers only in countries which requested them. However unfairly, almost inevitably its personnel and undertakings were nonetheless often considered tainted by association with American covert and overt military actions.

In practice, throughout the Cold War United States military assistance budgets, under the Mutual Security

Program inaugurated in 1951 and renewed annually thereafter, greatly outweighed spending on developmental aid. In Asia nationalist and insurgent movements, some Communist, some not, were strong in the Dutch East Indies (Indonesia), British Malaya, and French Indochina. In early 1950 the 'defense perimeter' strategy led the United States to furnish economic and military aid to Burma and Thailand. Leaving the British to tackle the Malayan emergency, in May 1950 the United States signed a military aid agreement to assist France and its Bao Dai puppet government in French Indochina. It was still uncertain whether the island of Taiwan, where the Chinese Nationalist government fled in 1949 and established a rump government-in-exile, would escape Communist conquest, but in late May 1950 American aid shipments to it were expedited.

The outbreak of the Korean War in June 1950 proved crucial both in implementing NSC 68 and in effectively globalizing the Cold War. Like Europe, Asia was experiencing rapid political and constitutional change. From 1945 to 1952 Japan, the former regional great power, defeated in war, was under United States occupation. Initially, officials in Washington, preoccupied with the evolving European situation, left the administration of Japan largely to the supreme commander of occupation forces, General Douglas MacArthur, who instituted extensive political and social reforms. As Communist victory in China appeared ever more probable, American officials began to view Japan as a potential bulwark of American power in Asia. Occupation policies now de-emphasized reform, focusing instead upon Japanese economic revival and association with the United States as an Asian offshore defence bastion. In 1951 the two countries concluded a security treaty, under which the military role of Japan remained severely limited but bases were to be provided for substantial numbers of United States troops.

The American decision to reintegrate Japan into the international system reflected the collapse of the wartime strategy of making China its primary Asian ally. From 1945 onwards the Nationalist regime of Jiang Jieshi (Chiang Kaishek) faced a serious Communist challenge led by Mao Zedong. Both sides resented American attempts in 1946 to mediate the conflict and establish a coalition government including the Communists as junior partners. From 1947 onwards it became increasingly apparent that a Communist regime would soon control the massive territory and population of China. When this occurred, Mao Zedong, who self-consciously perceived Chinese Communists as part of an international revolutionary movement, swiftly 'leaned to one side', favouring the Soviet Union, with which China signed a Treaty of Friendship and Alliance in January 1950.

Despite some past tensions between the Chinese Communists and Stalin, who had been prepared to tolerate a Nationalist government in China and extorted Chinese territorial and political concessions at Yalta, Mao viewed the United States as the ultimate enemy of China. American officials, especially Dean Acheson, Truman's influential secretary of state from 1949 to 1953, believed that ultimately Sino–Soviet tensions would cause China to break with the Soviet Union, as Yugoslavia did in 1948, and then turn to the United States. The interim United States response was to devise a 'great crescent' containment strategy of supporting non-Communist regimes and forces around China, from Pakistan, through Burma, Malaya, Thailand, present-day Indonesia, the Philippines, Indochina, and Japan.

In June 1950 North Korea (the Democratic People's Republic of Korea) invaded South Korea (the Republic of Korea). In 1945, when Soviet and American forces jointly liberated Korea from thirty-five years of Japanese occupation, they divided the country at the thirty-eighth parallel. As in Germany, occupation zones hardened into two separate states, the northern a Communist government led by Kim Il Sung, the southern a non-Communist authoritarian regime headed by Syngman Rhee. Each leader shared the objective of uniting all Korea under himself, and Kim's invasion was intended to accomplish this.

Stalin, who only endorsed the venture in the mistaken belief that the United States would not intervene, cautiously contributed military supplies but no Soviet personnel. In January 1950 Acheson had excluded South Korea from those Asian interests that the United States would defend militarily, but he and Truman now considered the invasion a Soviet test of American resolve. They succeeded in winning United Nations approval for military action to restore the status quo in Korea, an objective which the predominantly American UN troops, led by MacArthur, achieved by September 1950. Succumbing to hubris, American officials yielded to MacArthur's desire to conquer all Korea. After sweeping early victories which seemed to promise reunification by Christmas 1950, in November UN forces encountered Chinese 'volunteer' troops, who quickly reversed the tide of war and drove their opponents south. By spring 1951 the war had settled into a stalemate, ended by an armistice agreement in June 1953.

Korea had an enormous impact on the broader Cold War. American officials viewed the conflict not as a Korean civil war in which two small states rather adeptly manipulated more powerful patrons, but as proof positive that in Asia and globally the international Communist camp, effectively united under Soviet leadership, actively sought to expand its territory. United States defence spending soared in Europe as well as Asia, reaching $48 billion in fiscal 1951 and $61 billion the following year, and after the armistice still remained far higher than previously. In June 1950 the United States had 1,460,000 military personnel, of whom 280,000 were stationed abroad; four years later the totals were 3,555,000 and 963,000.

Fearing that Korea was only a feint intended to divert attention from a forthcoming threat to Europe, in late 1950 Truman sent four additional American divisions to join the two such under-strength formations already on the continent, a deployment which effectively soon became permanent. In 1951 a unified NATO command structure was created, headed by Dwight D. Eisenhower, the Second World War commander, and the politically and internationally controversial decision was taken to rearm West Germany within NATO.

These measures were only part of a broader expansion of American overseas commitments. American troops were stationed permanently in South Korea, and Rhee's price for accepting an armistice which left Korea divided was an American security treaty. The war likewise transformed the Republic of China on Taiwan from rather an embarrassment into an American ally, as the United States pledged itself to withhold the island from Communist China, in 1954 concluding a mutual defence treaty with Taiwan. Meanwhile, the United States denied mainland China diplomatic recognition and pressured its allies to do likewise and to refuse the People's Republic representation in the United Nations. In 1951, during the Korean war, the United States concluded the ANZUS defence pact, bringing Australia and New Zealand into its network of alliances and the Pacific security chain. The SEATO (Southeast Asian Treaty Organization) pact of 1954 completed the containing ring around China, including the United States, Britain, France, Australia, New Zealand, Thailand, the Philippines, and Pakistan in a mutual security alliance, and extending its protection to three non-member states, Laos, Cambodia, and Vietnam.

Despite American military assistance in French Indochina, after their defeat at Dienbienphu, which Vietminh nationalist forces inflicted on them in 1954, the French decided to jettison their former Asian colonies. Under the Geneva accords of 1954, three separate states were established. Vietnam was left partitioned between Communist and non-Communist forces in the north and south respectively, with countrywide elections for a single national government scheduled for 1956. Meanwhile, under President Ngo Dinh Diem the southern portion received enormous American economic and military aid, as did other non-Communist Asian states. When Communist or left-wing insurgency threatened, as with the Hukbalahap peasant rebellion in the Philippines in the mid-1950s, massive American assistance was usually offered to combat it. By contrast, governments the United States perceived as moving leftward could anticipate fierce American opposition. In 1949 the Dutch granted Indonesia independence, under substantial pressure from the United States, which supported the non-Communist authoritarian nationalist Ahmed Sukarno. In the mid-1950s Sukarno, a strong supporter of non-alignment, proposed including Communist Party representatives in the government and visited Moscow and Beijing, obtaining aid from both. The United States responded by providing covert military assistance, including the use of American aeroplanes and bases in the Philippines, to an unsuccessful 1958 rebellion by dissatisfied army officers.

Such blatant intervention was also common in Latin America. Since the early nineteenth century the United States had claimed a special position in the Western Hemisphere, warning non-American states against colonizing or intervening in the affairs of Latin American nations while demanding that those countries respect United States rights, interests, and concerns. Yankee imperialism, particularly the United States' tendency to coerce or even intervene militarily against its neighbours, was sometimes highly unpopular in the region, but these states were usually too comparatively weak to resist such hegemonic pressure. In the Cold War, the United States demanded that Latin

American nations adopt its own international outlook. In September 1947 nineteen joined the United States in signing the Rio Pact, the Inter-American Treaty of Reciprocal Assistance, which committed its members to join each other in resisting aggression, even from another signatory. The next year the Organization of American States was established, a hemispheric institution whose charter set out procedures for arbitrating disputes among members.

These agreements could, if necessary, be used to justify American intervention against southern neighbours liable to stray from the anti-Communist fold. The widespread poverty, deprivation, economic inequalities, and authoritarian political repression which characterized many Latin American nations, and the fact that in many cases United States economic interests benefited from and colluded with the established status quo in these countries, made United States intervention likely. Reformist governments which threatened United States interests could expect to be portrayed as pro-Communist and encounter United States hostility. Thus, in June 1953 the United States Central Intelligence Agency (CIA) helped to organize a coup which overthrew President Jacobo Arbenz Guzmán of Guatemala, a popularly elected leader who had instituted a programme of land reform which threatened properties owned by the United Fruit Company, a large American corporation. Vintage American aircraft flown by CIA pilots attacked the capital, and an authoritarian military junta replaced Arbenz.

This episode indicated the degree to which covert operations against supposedly independent states and collusion with authoritarian dictators came to characterize United States Cold War policies. It was also symptomatic of the pronounced United States tendency to conflate the defence of particular American interests with anti-Communism, in the process seriously damaging its own international credibility. To many on the left and in developing countries, United States protestations of liberal ideals and support for freedom and democracy appeared mere hypocritical propaganda rationalizing its imperialist economic and international exploitation of other countries.

Attempting to allay such suspicions while alleviating poverty, illiteracy, and disease, widely perceived as precipitating factors in Communist insurgencies in the region, in March 1961 the United States established the Alliance for Progress, a ten-year, $10 billion aid programme for Latin American nations, Cuba excepted. The administration hoped that this undertaking, designed to integrate the separate Latin American economies and promote annual growth rates of 2.5 per cent, fair wages, stable prices, agrarian reform, tax revision, housing development, health, sanitation, and literacy, would also facilitate the development of democratic governments to replace military dictatorships. Under Kennedy the programme brought merely a few marginal improvements, as growth rates reached only 1.5 per cent, illiteracy remained stable, per capita agricultural production declined, and unemployment rose. The Kennedy administration itself blocked reforms in Honduras which would have expropriated American-owned land holdings, and military coups overthrew no fewer than six popularly elected presidents.

Until the 1980s, the scarcity or absence of Latin American democratic governments led the United States to provide extensive military and economic assistance to indigenous military elites, authoritarian rulers prepared to protect American interests and characterize themselves as anti-Communist. When more radical regimes, whether revolutionary or popularly elected, emerged, they generally encountered United States opposition. Successive American presidents launched covert operations against Fidel Castro, who came to power in Cuba in 1959; sent troops to the Dominican Republic in 1965, to ensure that a supposedly radical army faction failed in a complicated civil war; and in the early 1970s successfully facilitated a coup against the popularly elected government of President Salvador Allende of Chile.

In the Middle East, where post-colonial nationalism was strong, the United States was likewise often perceived as representing conservative, illiberal forces opposing change, the successor of European imperialism. Indeed, the inability of Britain to maintain its pre-1945 regional hegemony in the Middle East, whose strategic advantages and oil resources American policymakers were determined to deny to the Soviets, was a major reason for United States involvement. Oil-rich Iran quickly attracted United States interest. In 1953 a radical government headed by Prime Minister Mohammed Mossadeq attempted to nationalize British oil interests in Iran and threatened to seek Soviet assistance should Dwight Eisenhower, the new American president, not endorse this policy. Supported by the youthful monarch of Iran, the pro-Western Shah Reza Pahlavi II, the Central Intelligence Agency organized a coup which overthrew Mossadeq and left real power to the shah.

For twenty-five years this authoritarian modern-day enlightened despot would be the keystone of American Middle Eastern policy, allocating American oil companies a 40 per cent stake in Iranian oil operations and receiving several billion dollars of American military and economic assistance. In addition to its Iranian alliance, the United States attempted to persuade other Arab states to collaborate against potential Soviet expansionism. In 1955 it encouraged the establishment of the Baghdad Pact, a grouping of Turkey, Iran, Iraq, Pakistan, and Britain, which established a military liaison with the United States. After Iraq, the only Arab member, withdrew in 1958, this metamorphosed into the Central Treaty Organization (CENTO), of which the United States became a full member.

A complicating factor in the Middle East was the support Truman – against the advice of his State Department – gave to the creation in 1948 of the separate Jewish state of Israel, whose elimination was for decades a unifying article of faith for the otherwise Muslim nations in the region. Immediately after the establishment of Israel, as it faced military attack from its Arab neighbours, the Soviet Union and the United States both recognized Israel and used massive arms shipments to compete for its allegiance. Caught between the passionate support American Jews gave Israel and their fear of further alienating resentful and oil-rich Arab states, whose anger might propel them towards the Soviets, in 1948 United States officials launched the first of many successive and still continuing efforts to negotiate a lasting Middle East peace settlement between Arabs and Israelis. Meanwhile, the strong domestic Jewish lobby ensured that the small, beleaguered Israeli state quickly became the single largest recipient of American military and economic aid, a virtual United States client.

American assistance to Israel, in turn, angered Arabs, particularly the more radical nationalist elements in the region's patchwork of rival states. Gamal Abdel Nasser, the young, anti-British president of Egypt, took power in 1952 determined to reverse decades of Western-inflicted Arab humiliation and to overthrow Israel. In 1955 he sought and obtained arms for this purpose from the Soviet bloc, which led the United States to withdraw promised economic assistance for a major hydroelectric project, the Aswan dam. Nasser then announced his intention to nationalize the strategic waterway the Suez Canal, still under British and French control, which gave ships quick passage from the Indian Ocean to the Mediterranean Sea, and use canal revenues to finance the dam project. He also established a pan-Arab alliance of Egypt, Saudi Arabia, Syria, and Yemen, later expanded to include other states.

Against American advice, in October 1956 the British, French, and Israelis jointly attacked Egypt, defeating its army, whereupon Nasser blocked the canal. Fearing a major oil crisis, permanent Middle Eastern instability, and the further strengthening of both radical nationalism and Soviet influence, Eisenhower demanded the invaders withdraw their forces, threatening to cease supporting the British currency should they refuse. The harsh American reaction caused great bitterness in Britain, underlining irrevocably that the once proud British empire was now a second-rate power, dependent on its American ally.

The Suez crisis coincided almost exactly with the brutal Soviet suppression in November 1956 of a Hungarian attempt to establish an independent, non-Communist government and leave the Warsaw Pact. Soviet readiness to use military force and kill thousands of Hungarians severely damaged Soviet Communism's international image and prestige, persuading many left-wing intellectuals to reject either Communism itself or at least Soviet dominance of the worldwide Communist movement. In Western Europe and the United States the Hungarian uprising precipitated the emergence of the New Left movement, a loose grouping of socialist and radical intellectuals who often retained their Marxist faith but were deeply sceptical towards or spurned Soviet pretensions to international Communist leadership. The contemporaneous criticism of many aspects of Stalin's leadership by his successor, Nikita Khrushchev, the new Soviet party secretary, further damaged Soviet claims to doctrinal infallibility, loosening the Russian grip on the loyalties of the international left.

Possibly hoping to distract international attention from Hungary, late in the Suez crisis Khrushchev interjected the Soviet Union into it. Although American pressure forced the invaders to back down, Khrushchev attempted to divert the credit for this to his own country by threatening rocket attacks on Britain, France, and Israel unless they withdrew. Given the limited Soviet nuclear arsenal, this threat was almost certainly empty bluff, but it was made sufficiently close to the cease-fire to enable Khrushchev to claim responsibility.

Fearing that Khrushchev's intervention heralded enhanced Soviet 'subversive activities' in the region, in January 1957 Eisenhower sought congressional authority not only to increase economic and military aid to anti-Soviet Middle Eastern states but also to use military force against 'overt armed aggression from any nation controlled by International Communism'. Arab states immediately condemned the 'Eisenhower Doctrine', under whose auspices the United States successfully intervened in both Lebanon and Jordan in 1958 to shore up pro-Western governments. Thus, although during the Suez crisis the United States had aligned itself firmly with nationalist anti-colonial forces, its prevailing image among Middle Eastern states remained that of a conservative, imperialist power, a perception that subsequent American actions had reinforced.

In Africa, where many colonies gained their independence by the mid-1960s, opposing Cold War camps cautiously attempted to recruit them, generally offering economic aid packages. Africa ranked low in American priorities. The United States tended to defer to the wishes of the colonial powers, its European allies, and avoided overly close identification with nationalist movements. To many Africans American readiness to tolerate continued white rule in South Africa as preferable to possible disorder and Communist infiltration, and to acquiesce in Portuguese colonialism in Angola in exchange for naval bases in the Azores, discredited the United States. Symbolic American protests on Angola and South Africa did little to remedy the situation.

Alhough they did not anticipate especially warm relations with most African states, American officials nonetheless hoped at least to deny Africa to the Soviets. African nations were often neutralist in orientation, and under Kennedy American officials attempted to use economic aid to entice such countries as Kwame Nkrumah's Ghana into the pro-Western camp. Until the 1970s the Congo (Zaire) crisis of 1960–1961, when the Soviets backed a left-wing secessionist movement in Katanga province while the United States supported efforts by United Nations peacekeeping forces to restore order and maintain pro-Western leaders in power, was the most significant episode in which Cold War rivalries affected African affairs. Soviet missions were not particularly popular in Africa, where Communist Chinese representatives, drawing on a shared sense of difference from and resentment of all Western powers, the Soviets included, proved more effective in conscious competition with their Communist rivals to win friends and influence.

Soviet attempts to gain international leverage tended to be less systematic than the global network of United States alliances, partners, and clients. The Soviets avoided direct military confrontation with Western powers or uncompromising alliance commitments which might have obliged them to take such action. Instead, they relied upon military and economic assistance, although even in this area Soviet economic inferiority to the United States restricted its ability to compete. Ideologically, the picture was different. Despite the New Left's post-Hungary disillusionment, to many non-Western nations and individuals the Soviet system appeared to command the international moral high ground, representing a form of government more altruistic, generous, and idealistic than Western capitalism. In the 1950s and 1960s the Soviets displayed real enthusiasm for individual third world leaders of national liberation movements, such as Nasser and Sukarno, only on occasion to be embarrassingly disillusioned, as in 1958, when Nasser brutally suppressed domestic Communists, a course his rival, the Iraqi dictator Abdul Karim Kassem, imitated the following year. In 1972 the Egyptians again disappointed them, expelling most of the Soviet military advisers who had assisted Egypt after its defeat in the 1967 Six Day War.

Some states, such as Egypt and on occasion India, cleverly played the two superpowers against each other, extracting substantial assistance from each. The conscious emergence from the early 1950s of a 'non-aligned movement' of states associated with neither major Cold War protagonist facilitated such strategies. As early as 1946 Mao Zedong suggested there existed a 'vast intermediate zone', to which China belonged, of countries which professed allegiance to neither Cold War superpower. John Foster Dulles, American secretary of state from 1953 to 1959, repeatedly proclaimed what he characterized as the 'immorality of neutrality': that the issues involved in the Soviet–American international rivalry were of such overwhelming concern to all that no nation could be justified in trying to remain aloof from it. Many nations, particularly post-colonial developing states, disagreed entirely and wished to escape such bipolar rigidities.

A formal Non-Aligned Movement was only established in the 1970s, but *ad hoc* conferences were held at symbolically important locations: Bandung (Indonesia) in 1955, Belgrade (Yugoslavia) in 1961, and Cairo (Egypt) in 1962. India and Egypt led the movement, which attracted Communist mavericks such as Yugoslavia and numerous Asian, African, and Latin American countries. They tended to focus primarily upon post-colonial issues and the problems developing economies shared. Reflecting a certain geographic and psychological distance from Eurocentric Cold War preoccupations, and for China perhaps also growing Sino–Soviet dissension, even China and Japan sent representatives to these meetings. From the mid-1950s the Soviet Union, following a pragmatic united front rationale that treated as friendly any country not allied with the West, endorsed the movement. Indeed, a state such as India, democratic but socialist in political orientation, especially given that its sworn enemy Pakistan received extensive American military assistance, might well tilt towards the Soviet side in specific international disputes even as it professed formal Cold War neutrality.

Determined to win the Cold War and to prevent further Communist gains in developing areas, in the 1950s and 1960s the United States deliberately disparaged neutralist efforts and sought to prevent what it perceived as the weakening of the free world consequent on the loss of any non-Communist territory. These preoccupations led to American involvement in the Vietnam War, the logical consequence of the Truman Doctrine and the most traumatically disastrous military experience in United States history. After the French left Indochina in 1954, the southern Republic of Vietnam effectively became an American client, attracting heavy infusions of military and economic aid. Fearing that the northern-based Communists led by Ho Chi Minh would win nationwide elections scheduled for 1956, the United States urged its client government under President Ngo Dinh Diem to refuse to hold these, on the grounds that the Vietnamese Communists had broken various Geneva accord provisions. In the late 1950s the northern Democratic Republic of Vietnam launched increasingly serious Viet Cong guerrilla attacks against the south. The United States, eager to support a client and erroneously characterizing the decidedly independent-minded Vietnamese Communists as Chinese puppets, increased assistance to South Vietnam.

Three successive American presidents, Eisenhower, Kennedy, and Lyndon B. Johnson, steadily escalated the war. Under Kennedy the number of American military advisers rose from 600 to 16,000. Although the United States never formally declared war, after Congress passed the Tonkin Gulf resolution of August 1964, giving him a mandate to take whatever action he considered appropriate, Johnson not only launched extensive bombing raids on the north, but from 1965 committed ever greater numbers of American ground troops. By 1967 American forces in Vietnam totalled 436,000. The north obtained military and economic assistance from both mainland China and the Soviet Union. All three great powers involved feared the situation might spiral out of control into outright war with each other, an outcome they sought to avoid through covert signalling among themselves. On both sides, a small client Vietnamese state showed considerable skill in manipulating larger and more powerful allies to its own ends.

In January 1968 Viet Cong forces initiated the Tet offensive, a countrywide attempt to defeat the Americans, and although the effort failed, its scale – along with successful guerrilla incursions even into the grounds of the United States embassy in Saigon, the southern capital – convinced many Americans, including senior presidential advisers, that the war was unwinnable. In March Johnson announced he would seek a negotiated peace settlement, preferably one which would maintain South Vietnam as a viable state. Not until 1973 did his Republican successor, Richard Nixon, obtain such an agreement, at the price of permitting North Vietnamese forces to retain their existing positions in the south, but this did not settle matters. Two years later, in 1975, northern forces invaded the south, overran it within a few weeks, and unified Vietnam, their goal since 1945. The Americans withdrew, but it was not until 1995 that the United States recognized the new socialist government of Vietnam, for two decades deliberately denying it economic assistance from international agencies to which the United States belonged.

The effective defeat in Vietnam, a small now devastated country, severely threatened American self-confidence. Within the United States ferocious anti-war protests, particularly by the young, generated serious social and political tensions and led many to question the entire underlying rationale and legitimacy of United States policies since 1945. The violent United States prosecution of war against a small, weak, third-world nation, well-publicized atrocities, and the corrupt and undemocratic nature of the South Vietnamese government, impelled many Americans to doubt the intrinsic morality, not just of this particular commitment, but of the entire containment policy which had guided their country since the late 1940s. Revelations of Cold War excesses by top American officials, including the secret bombing of Cambodia and Laos between 1969 and 1971, deliberate international and internal deception and misrepresentation, covert operations against other nations, and internal espionage, damaged government credibility. The massively expensive Vietnam commitment fuelled rising American inflation, and the serious economic problems which afflicted the country in the 1970s generated pressures to cut defence spending. For the rest of the century American officials were exceedingly cautious in committing troops overseas, fearing that even relatively low casualty figures might generate severe political damage. The war also helped to impel American leaders to seek a new rapprochement with both China and the Soviet Union.

THREE

The Quest for Superpower Understanding, 1953–1974

Their sworn antagonism notwithstanding, in practice the Soviet Union and the United States shared certain common interests. As both acquired nuclear and then thermonuclear weapons, despite the extreme rhetoric their leaders frequently employed, in practice moderation became essential to prevent a situation which might, even inadvertently, lead them to detonate atomic warheads. Soviet and American leaders hoped to prevent the acquisition of nuclear weapons by other powers, thereby assuring themselves and two close American allies, Britain and France, an effective monopoly. Heavy military spending imposed severe budgetary burdens on both superpowers, which from the 1950s onwards they sought to alleviate. In March 1953 Stalin, the feared tyrant who had dominated Soviet politics, died. Though cautious in dealing with Western powers and unwilling to permit Soviet troops to risk direct military confrontation with them, Stalin never seriously trusted the West and jovially encouraged China to embroil the United States in such costly conflicts as Korea. His demise freed his successors to be more accommodating.

Nikita Khrushchev, emerging triumphant in 1955 from internal Kremlin power struggles, repudiated much of the legacy of Stalin. In February 1956, in a secret seven-hour speech to the Soviet presidium, of which Western intelligence agencies quickly obtained a fairly reliable transcript, he condemned Stalin's unfettered personal power, his use of terror, and the leadership cult he erected around himself. Khrushchev also suggested that Stalin's personal conduct of diplomacy often threatened peace with other nations. Although inalterably committed to Communism and firmly believing his political system would ultimately triumph, from 1956 onwards the sometimes erratic Khrushchev sought a certain understanding with Western powers, ensuring their 'peaceful coexistence'. Khrushchev argued that war between the Communist and capitalist camps was no longer inevitable, and that socialism might on occasion advance through tactics of peaceful evolution rather than violent revolution.

In 1958 Khrushchev even felt sufficiently secure to renounce the traditional Soviet dogma that hostile capitalist states encircled the Communist world, arguing one could no longer state 'who encircles whom, the capitalist countries the socialist states, or vice versa'. He took this line partly because, despite substantial internal military opposition, he wished to divert the Soviet economy from heavy industry and defence spending towards light industry, agriculture, and consumer goods. He therefore chose to place greater emphasis upon nuclear weapons and less upon more costly conventional armed forces. The successful Soviet explosion of a hydrogen bomb in 1955 and of high-yield thermonuclear weapons in 1957, and its triumphs launching the first inter-continental ballistic missile and boosting Sputnik, the first man-made space satellite, into orbit in 1957 were spec-tacular public relations coups which apparently proved his strategy successful. In reality, Khrushchev's public utter-ances greatly exaggerated the Russian nuclear stockpile; even in 1962, the Soviets only possessed around twenty missiles capable of reaching United States territory, and overall the Americans enjoyed an eighteenfold advantage in warheads targeted on the Soviet Union as opposed to Soviet weapons aimed at the United States.

To American leaders budgetary considerations were also important. On becoming president in 1953, Eisenhower introduced the 'New Look' strategic doctrine, which likewise relied heavily on nuclear weapons rather than costlier conventional military forces. Secretary of state Dulles emphasized that his country would adopt policies of 'massive retaliation' in any international crisis, reinforcing fears already widespread during the Korean War that the United States might risk international nuclear destruction over a relatively trivial incident. These tactics could easily lead to 'brinkmanship', a strategy whereby the United States, apparently at least, approached the verge of nuclear war during various international crises. Eisenhower's seeming threat in 1953 to use nuclear weapons should no armistice end the continuing Korean War and his discussion in 1954 of their potential employment to preserve the increasingly desperate French position in Indochina alarmed many in the West. The successive Taiwan straits crises of 1954–1955 and 1958, when the United States appeared to contemplate employing atomic weapons to prevent mainland China taking two small Taiwan-held islands near its coast, further stoked such fears. So, too, did a sabre-rattling crisis over Berlin which erupted sporadically from late 1958, when Khrushchev began attempts to stem a costly haemorrhage of East German professionals to the Federal Republic by annexing the Western sector of Berlin, until 1961, when he resolved the problem by constructing the notorious Berlin Wall. Apparently, Eisenhower and Dulles were in reality more cautious than their rhetoric implied, but in the United States and Europe these various episodes helped to precipitate a strong anti-nuclear movement, the Campaign for Nuclear Disarmament.

The strength of anti-nuclear fears indicated that American attempts rigorously to enforce domestic anti-Communist orthodoxy were somewhat unsuccessful. In the early 1950s followers of the fiercely anti-Communist Senator Joseph McCarthy of Wisconsin, who alleged Communist agents had infiltrated the entire American apparatus of government, including the presidency and the foreign policy bureaucracy, attracted much support. Capitalizing on popular frustration over Communist victory in China and the stalemated Korean War and on the sense of menace which Soviet possession of devastating atomic weapons engendered in the American public, McCarthy assailed many Truman administration officials, including secretaries of state Marshall and Acheson, as Communist traitors. In the 1952 presidential election campaign Eisenhower chose the politically advantageous course of refusing publicly to condemn these tactics.

Throughout the 1950s, they helped to generate an atmosphere of ferocious anti-Communist hysteria in the United States, demonizing the enemy as all powerful and omnipresent. Ironically, this approach subverted many of the values of democracy, liberty, and individual rights the United States purported to defend. For some years an un-proved, even undocumented accusation of pro-Com-munist or leftist sympathies could easily suffice to ruin a once promising career. The Federal Bureau of Investiga-tion implemented a broad, generally unconstitutional programme of domestic surveillance. Internally American politicians also tended to use Cold War considerations to enforce conformity, arguing, for example, that to highlight or attempt to remedy such sources of domestic discontent as the heavy disabilities black Americans experienced or the dissatisfaction of women with the restrictions they faced would weaken the existing American social fabric, thereby aiding and comforting the ever-present enemy.

Countries other than the United States used Cold War priorities to enforce internal conformity. Such tactics were popular both throughout the Communist bloc and in countries allied with the West. Kennan had already accurately suggested that Soviet politicians could justify their harsh rule and the deprivations their citizens endured by proclaiming that resistance to external threats demanded these. In mainland China and North Korea, Communist leaders utilized the Korean War and anti-American sentiment to justify domestic repression, capitalizing on the conflict and the calls for patriotism it generated to eliminate potential political opposition or dissent. Later Mao Zedong habitually invoked foreign threats to justify similar repressive efforts, including the Hundred Flowers campaign of 1958 and the Great Proletarian Cultural Revolution of the late 1960s, as did Kim Il Sung in North Korea. In Taiwan, South Korea, and numerous other American allies, domestic intolerance was harsh and Cold War and national security considerations were normally cited in its defence. The Soviets likewise portrayed their successive interventions to suppress 'deviationist' regimes in Eastern Europe as measures necessary to defend international Communism. Even in the more libertarian West European nations, governments and security forces often ignored civil rights, claiming overriding Cold War interests were at stake.

At least some people in the Eisenhower administration, including the president, were apprehensive that, in the quest for Cold War victory, the values their country claimed to represent would be ignored or destroyed. As an incontrovertible military hero, Eisenhower was inoculated against potential domestic criticism that he was selling out to Communism. His own perennial fear, most famously expressed in his 1961 Farewell Address, was that permanently high levels of defence spending and taxation would prove detrimental to American democracy; and his concern for governmental economy and his sense that it was desirable that American overseas commitments and the 'military-industrial complex' should be scaled back in 'the foreseeable future', impelled him to seek an understanding with the Soviets. Moreover, while aware that the Soviet nuclear arsenal was vastly inferior to the American, Eisenhower also recognized that even the relatively small number of Russian missiles which would escape a Western first strike might wreak enormous, possibly unsurvivable, devastation. He hoped that the balance of terror would persuade both antagonists to refrain from war, a hope that inspired the famed acronym 'MAD', standing for Mutually Assured Destruction.

The elderly Churchill, restored to power as British prime minister from 1951 to 1954, reinforced this message, urging his former wartime associate Eisenhower to relax nuclear tensions and seek Soviet–American rapprochement. During the Korean War the British repeatedly attempted to moderate both United States suggestions that the use of nuclear weapons against China and North Korea might be acceptable, and overly harsh American rhetoric in the United Nations regarding its opponents. Dulles' hard-line emphasis on massive retaliation and on the 'roll back' of Communism in Eastern Europe alarmed the British, who feared that his actions might provoke nuclear war. Their pressure proved unable to counteract the influence of Dulles and other State Department officials who feared that such an understanding would gravely weaken the Western alliance, and who shared West German Chancellor Konrad Adenauer's belief that the full integration of West Germany into the NATO military structure was essential to West European security. As with Suez, given Britain's near unwavering public support for American policies, its failure to affect Dulles' stance clearly indicated the extent of United States dominance of its Cold War allies and how profoundly, by the 1950s, British power had diminished.

Even so, throughout his presidency Eisenhower sought, albeit with only partial success, to improve Soviet–American relations. On various occasions Soviet and United States actions alike compromised such endeavours. Immediately after Stalin's death, American officials contemplated four-power talks among themselves, the Soviets, Britain, and France to settle outstanding questions, including the future of Germany. Schemes for potential German unification and neutralization were even floated, although Eisenhower and Dulles were unenthusiastic. In July the brutal Soviet suppression of a workers' uprising in East Berlin temporarily blighted all hopes for understanding, with the Eisenhower administration ignoring the opportunity to follow through on earlier campaign promises to 'roll back' Communism in Eastern Europe, and restricting its support for East Germany to propaganda and food aid.

A Soviet–American public relations battle brought little tangible result. In late 1953 Eisenhower made an

'Atoms for Peace' proposal, suggesting that nuclear powers should donate fissionable materials to an international agency which would develop and use atomic energy for peaceable purposes. As in the past, the Soviets responded by suggesting a joint declaration renouncing and banning atomic weapons. In 1955 the four occupation powers did succeed in negotiating an agreement to withdraw all foreign forces from Austria, leaving the country neutralized, allied to neither Cold War protagonist. It proved impossible to reach a similar arrangement in Germany, the strongest economy in Europe and – particularly if united – potentially the greatest military power, since neither great power was prepared to risk such a major asset attaching itself to the opposing camp.

The Austrian settlement did bring a summit meeting of British, American, and Soviet leaders at Geneva in July 1955, its agenda potential schemes for disarmament and the reduction of nuclear weapons. Disarmament proposals foundered on Soviet attempts to make these conditional on the withdrawal of American troops from Europe, massive reductions in NATO forces, or German neutralization, all unacceptable to the Western powers. Eisenhower suggested instead that each side should permit free aerial inspection by the other of its military bases, to ensure that agreed armament limits were observed, but the Soviets refused, fearing that this 'open skies' policy would merely apprise their opponents of the exact location of their military installations which nuclear weapons could then target. By mid-1956 the United States had secretly developed and put into service U-2 spy planes, equipped with high resolution camera equipment and capable of conducting surveillance missions from 14 miles above Soviet territory. These techniques enabled Eisenhower to assure himself that, notwithstanding grandiose Soviet propaganda and allegations by political rivals that a missile gap existed, the American nuclear stockpile far surpassed the Soviet.

In October 1956 the brutal Soviet suppression of the student-led revolution in their East European satellite of Hungary, which ended in the mass execution of the Hungarian prime minister, Imre Nagy, his cabinet, and thousands of others, temporarily dissipated Soviet–American cordiality. Yet once again, the United States offered the dissidents only rhetorical support, accepting exiles and refugees but refusing to risk nuclear war by intervening. The Soviet Union subsequently increased economic aid to its European satellites, hoping thereby to pre-empt future demands for independence.

However strained relations were, neither side could afford to ignore nuclear issues. In 1957 the Soviet Union, having successfully developed thermonuclear weapons, delivery vehicles, and satellites, proposed a ban on nuclear testing. For six months in 1958 Russia unilaterally observed such a moratorium, requesting Britain and the United States, the other nuclear powers, to follow suit. The end of the moratorium subjected the Western powers to such public pressure that for three years, from November 1958, no nuclear tests took place.

Negotiations for a test ban treaty began concurrently, but soon deadlocked over inspection provisions.

Before leaving office in early 1961 Eisenhower hoped to sign a test ban treaty with Khrushchev and to settle the continuing dispute over West Berlin, which Khrushchev claimed should be entirely under East German control. In 1960 the two superpowers and Britain progressed steadily towards acceptable treaty terms, expecting to finalize the agreement at a May 1960 Paris summit meeting between Eisenhower and Khrushchev. Early that month, however, the Soviets shot down an American U-2 surveillance plane deep over Soviet territory, capturing the pilot alive and inducing him to admit publicly he was on an espionage mission. Ignoring Soviet hints that he should disavow knowledge of the operation, Eisenhower took full responsibility, declining either to promise to cease all such flights or publicly to apologize. An atmosphere of acute hostility pervaded the summit, which Eisenhower left after two days. The only arms control agreement reached under Eisenhower was a December 1959 treaty whereby twelve countries, including Britain, France, the Soviet Union, and the United States, agreed to demilitarize the Antarctic and refrain from dumping radioactive wastes on the continent.

Under Kennedy, who succeeded Eisenhower, efforts for a test ban treaty continued, reaching fruition only after the Cold War's most serious nuclear crisis. Kennedy's initial dealings with Khrushchev were fraught, as problems erupted in Berlin and Laos. At a June 1961 summit meeting in Vienna, Kennedy unsuccessfully attempted to persuade Khrushchev to accept a status quo policy whereby each great power would respect the interests of the other. The next month, when Khrushchev demanded that the West withdraw its military forces from Berlin and started to construct the Berlin Wall, Kennedy responded by dispatching 1,500 additional American soldiers to the city by road across East German territory. The Berlin crisis eventually fizzled out, but this episode and growing Communist insurgencies in Vietnam and Laos impelled Kennedy to adopt a 'flexible response' strategy, whereby the United States expanded its nuclear arsenal substantially during the 1960s, but also enhanced its non-nuclear conventional capabilities to meet any international challenge. Kennedy feared that otherwise a relatively minor incident might quickly cross the nuclear threshold. Kennedy's new approach envisaged greater reliance on counterinsurgency forces trained in guerrilla warfare to supplement the covert actions and diplomacy already habitually employed in crisès.

In October 1962 U-2 reconnaissance planes gave Kennedy an opportunity to test his new tactics, when they provided photographic evidence that the Soviets had installed intermediate-range nuclear weapons on the island of Cuba, little more than a hundred miles from the American coast. In 1958 an indigenous revolutionary movement led by Fidel Castro seized power from Fulgencio Batista, dictator of Cuba since 1933 and a United States client. Although Castro initially declared he was not a Communist, from spring 1959 he covertly sought Soviet aid and military protection, and American economic pressure and boycotts quickly gave him an excuse to move openly into the Soviet camp. In response, the Central Intelligence Agency instituted a scheme to assist Cuban exiles to attack the island and overthrow Castro. Initiated under Eisenhower and inherited by Kennedy, the March 1961 Bay of Pigs invasion attempt proved a humiliating fiasco for the United States. Kennedy and his advisers continued to devise plans, often both ingenious and far-fetched, to overthrow Castro, who not unnaturally sought further Soviet succour.

In mid-1961, as the Berlin crisis intensified, military hard-liners in the Kremlin, frustrated for several years, succeeded in implementing major increases of 34 per cent in spending on conventional forces. Both the Bay of Pigs and Kennedy's bellicose inauguration rhetoric that his country would 'pay any price, bear any burden, meet any hardship, support any friend, oppose any foe to assure the survival and success of liberty' may have energized them. The recent United States deployment of intermediate-range missiles in Turkey, which threatened Soviet territory, further angered Khrushchev. It seems that he also hoped to pressure the United States to make concessions on Berlin. In addition, he apparently felt a romantic sense of solidarity with the new, revolutionary Cuban state, which reassured him and other old Communists that their cause still had international vitality. He therefore offered Soviet nuclear missiles, under the control of Soviet technicians and troops, to Castro, who accepted and oversaw their installation.

Whatever the logical justification for Khrushchev's behaviour, politically it would have been almost impossible for any American president to accept the situation. In 1962 the Cuban missiles would have doubled or even trebled the number of Soviet warheads targeted on the United States. When American officials discovered their presence, they demanded that the Soviet Union remove them, and announced a naval blockade or 'quarantine' around the island. After some hesitation Khrushchev agreed to do so, secretly obtaining an unpublicized pledge that the United States would shortly do likewise with the Turkish Jupiters. The United States also promised not to mount another invasion of Cuba.

Recently released tapes of conversations among Kennedy and his advisers reveal that, to avoid nuclear war, he was if necessary prepared to make even greater concessions to the Soviets. Showing considerable states-manship, he deliberately refrained from emphasizing the humiliation of Khrushchev. Yet new documentary evidence also reveals that the Cuban situation was even more critical than most involved then realized. American officials underestimated by a factor of four the number of Soviet troops on the island, and failed to realize that 158 warheads on the island, which Castro urged should be used if the United States were to invade, were already operational. Forty-two of them could have reached American territory. The potential for a panicky or triggerhappy military officer to spark a full-scale nuclear war almost certainly existed, retrospectively chilling evidence of the dangers inherent in these weapons.

The Cuban missile crisis had a sobering impact on its protagonists. Humiliation at American hands impelled Soviet leaders to instigate an expensive major nuclear build-up to achieve parity with the United States, reaching this in 1970. The fall from power of Khrushchev in 1964 was probably at least partly due to the missile crisis. On Kennedy it exerted a certain salutary maturing effect, leading the once brash young president strongly to advocate disarmament in the final months before his untimely death in November 1963. His stance impelled the Soviet leadership to establish a teletype 'hot line' between Moscow and Washington, to facilitate communications and ease tensions during international crises. The two powers also finally reached agreement on the limited test ban treaty, ratified in October 1963, which had been hanging fire for several years, so ending atmospheric testing of nuclear weapons.

One potential nuclear power declining to sign this agreement was the People's Republic of China, which was developing its own nuclear programme. Both Americans and Russians cherished some faint hopes that ratifying the treaty might conceivably dissuade China from joining the nuclear club. There are some indications that the Kennedy administration even hinted fruitlessly to Moscow that the United States would not object should the Soviets choose to bomb Chinese nuclear installations, destroying their developing programme. That this possibility could even be raised was conclusive evidence of the degree to which Sino–Soviet relations had deteriorated, fulfilling Acheson's

1949 prediction that within six to twelve years the Communist alliance would collapse. Both ideological and practical differences precipitated the Sino–Soviet split, which became public in October 1961 at the Twenty-Second Soviet Party congress. Tensions between Soviet and Chinese national interests had characterized the relationship since well before Mao attained power in China. Soviet reluctance to give wholehearted backing to China or risk nuclear war during the Taiwan straits crises, particularly that of 1958, galled the Chinese, as did the Soviet tilt towards India in the 1959 Sino–Indian border crisis. Chinese officials constantly criticized the poor quality of many Russian economic aid items. Soviet advisers deplored the disastrous Great Leap Forward economic programme which China launched in 1958. As tensions grew, in 1960 the Soviet Union unilaterally abrogated its Chinese aid programmes, withdrawing all its remaining experts and advisers.

On the ideological front, Mao found Khrushchev's denunciation of Stalin and his readiness to embrace peaceful coexistence with the United States virtual heresy, revisionist backsliding from the international Communist cause. The Chinese increasingly presented themselves as guardians of the true Communist faith. By the late 1950s Mao was increasingly preoccupied with defining a personal, highly revolutionary brand of Communism which made even many of his colleagues uncomfortable and reached its apogee in the late 1960s in the Great Proletarian Cultural Revolution. The Soviets considered Chinese readiness to risk nuclear confrontation with the Americans foolhardy adventurism. Dissension climaxed over the Chinese nuclear programme, which the Soviet Union assisted in the early 1950s. China was determined to acquire an independent nuclear capability. Initially, in October 1957, Soviet officials promised substantial technical and material assistance, but they quickly insisted that all weapons must remain under Soviet control, and in 1959 they abrogated the entire agreement. Chinese leaders characterized the gradual warming in Soviet–American relations and the nuclear test ban treaties as joint hegemonic attempts to maintain an international monopoly of power and nuclear weaponry. By 1962 relations between the two great Communist powers were almost unrelievedly hostile, and Soviet 'revisionist' influences became a major Cultural Revolution target.

The Sino–Soviet split gave the United States an opportunity to play the two leading Communist powers against each other, to its own advantage. American preoccupation with the widening Vietnam War, in which both China and the Soviet Union, eager to burnish their Communist leadership credentials, gave North Vietnam substantial military and economic assistance, postponed this development until the late 1960s. Each Communist power sought to gain strategic advantage and protection against its rival by moving closer to the United States. American officials, primarily President Richard Nixon and Henry A. Kissinger, his national security adviser (later secretary of state), sought to enhance the eroded United States international position. Kissinger and

Nixon consciously sought to create a new, in many ways traditional, structure of international relations which would incorporate the Soviet Union as a nonrevolutionary power, inducing it to exhibit new moderation and restraint. Conscious that their country no longer enjoyed the undisputed supremacy of the immediate post-1945 period and that growing economic difficulties necessitated cuts in defence budgets, they hoped to negotiate arms limitations agreements with the Soviet Union rather than unilaterally reducing American military spending. The Nixon Doctrine, announced in July 1969, called upon American allies to bear the primary burden of their own defence, looking to the United States only for supplementary conventional and, when necessary, nuclear assistance.

In Vietnam, this brought a new strategy of 'Vietnamization', gradually reducing American forces while furnishing South Vietnam massive military aid in the expectation its own troops would take up the slack. Nixon also stated that his country should be prepared only to fight one and a half wars, one major superpower confrontation plus a limited war such as Vietnam, rather than its former standard of two and a half wars. His new definition implied that the United States no longer anticipated armed hostilities with China.

Embroiled in a politically disastrous, unwinnable war in Vietnam, American leaders hoped that both big Communist powers would pressure North Vietnam to reach a peace settlement the United States could tolerate. A strategic understanding with China would enhance American ability to manipulate the Soviets, while Soviet–American détente would, it was hoped, make the Chinese Communists more accommodating, as both Communist rivals courted their former principal enemy.

The thaw in Sino–American relations preceded and helped to precipitate deténte with Russia. Predictably, Chinese leaders found highly alarming the 'Brezhnev Doctrine', proclaimed in August 1968 when Soviet troops entered Czechoslovakia and overthrew an overly independent satellite government, that the Soviet Union reserved the right to intervene by military force when Soviet leaders believed the interests of international Communism were threatened. In March 1969 Sino–Soviet border tensions escalated into serious military clashes along the Ussuri River on China's north-west frontier. Although Chinese troops were the aggressors, they sought outside international support against potential Soviet retaliation. In the 1960s American elite and public opinion moved steadily towards reopening diplomatic relations with the People's Republic, whose status as the legal government of China the United States had never recognized. In 1967, eighteen months before he became president, Nixon wrote a well-publicized article suggesting such recognition was becoming desirable. In an ironic reversal of their respective positions earlier in the decade, in mid-1969 Soviet leaders sent out feelers to discover the likely United States reaction should Russian missiles target and destroy Chinese nuclear installations, receiving an unambiguously discouraging American response. As a further deterrent, in October 1969 Nixon quietly put the Strategic Air Command on the highest level of nuclear alert, a warning the United States would not tolerate a nuclear attack on China. Sino–Soviet negotiations which ultimately resolved the Ussuri River crisis began shortly afterwards.

In a complicated minuet, Chinese and American leaders reciprocally signalled to each other their readiness to begin the process of reopening relations. From 1969 American loosening of travel and trade bans and the reduction of American naval and air patrols against China formed a counterpoint to confidential diplomatic contacts, culminating in July 1971 in a Kissinger secret visit to Beijing, the Chinese capital. Kissinger and Zhou Enlai, the Chinese prime minister, succeeded in resolving, at least provisionally, several outstanding contentious Sino–American issues, reaching guidelines they hoped would be used to decide the future of Vietnam and the status of Taiwan, still an American client. The following year Nixon visited China, signing a joint Sino–American communiqué on Taiwan, and in 1973 the United States and China opened liaison offices in each other's capitals. These were upgraded to embassies in 1979, when the United States broke relations with Taiwan, the two countries accorded each other full diplomatic recognition, and the United States concurrently granted China most-favoured-nation trading status.

For most of the 1970s the Sino–American relationship remained somewhat problematic. Within China the

'Gang of Four' radical faction centring on Mao's wife, Jiang Jing, disliked and sought to sabotage the pragmatic opening to the West, but their overthrow, which occurred shortly after Mao died in 1976, and was preceded by several years of bitter infighting, gave power to more pro-American elements, headed by Deng Xiaoping. In the early years of the relationship American reluctance to abandon Taiwan and Chinese resentment of its concurrent pursuit of détente with the Soviet Union also restrained further speedy warming. Even so, for both Americans and Chinese the resumption of relations marked a new era when the bipolar norms which originally characterized the post-1945 international system seemed increasingly irrelevant.

The American opening to China itself spurred the Soviet Union to move towards détente. By 1971 Russia had achieved nuclear parity with the United States, but only at a substantial economic price. If the United States continued to augment its arsenals, the Soviets would once more fall behind. Providing aid to North Vietnam was also expensive. In the late 1960s the Soviet economy experienced serious difficulties, including declining industrial growth and poor agricultural production. Improved relations with the West might well bring tangible benefits, including access to badly needed Western goods, technology, and even economic assistance, to the entire European Soviet bloc. The Soviets also feared their hold on East European loyalties was slipping, another incentive to improve relations with the West.

European allies of the United States, alarmed by its preoccupation with Vietnam and perceived neglect of their own concerns, were also likely to welcome détente with the Soviet Union, which would alleviate tensions on the European continent and also complement the *Ostpolitik* policies of closer relations between West Germany and its Communist neighbours that Willy Brandt, the first Social Democratic chancellor of the Federal Republic, spearheaded in the late 1960s. West Germany moved decisively to normalize dealings with countries which had previously refused to recognize it, between 1967 and 1974 establishing diplomatic relations with Rumania, Yugoslavia, Poland, Czechoslavakia, Bulgaria, and Hungary. In 1970 the Federal Republic accepted the existing borders of Poland, which incorporated territory that had until 1945 been German. Treaties with the Soviet Union in 1970 and East Germany in 1973 ratified the existing European borders and renounced the use of force to rectify them, even while leaving open the possibility of future German reunification.

Nixon and Kissinger would have preferred that Brandt move more slowly, facilitating their ability to extract concessions ('linkage') on Berlin, Indochina, and the Middle East from the Soviet Union in exchange for arms reduction, but he left them no choice. Minor arms control treaties proceeded apace: the Joint Space Mission Agreement of October 1970; a February 1971 understanding banning the siting of nuclear weapons on the ocean floor; and the September 1971 Agreement on

Measures to Reduce the Risk of Accidental Outbreak of Nuclear War. In August 1971 the Quadripartite Treaty on Berlin recognized West Berlin as part of West Germany, guaranteed Western powers unimpeded access between the Federal Republic and the city, and allowed West Berliners to visit the East. In May 1971 the Nixon administration agreed to sell the Soviets grain worth $136 million and to request the United States Congress to grant the Soviet Union most-favoured-nation trading status. Even though, in the Indo–Pakistani war of late 1971, when India assisted East Pakistan (present-day Bangladesh) to secede from Pakistan, the United States and China supported Pakistan while the Soviets favoured India, progress towards a Soviet–American Moscow summit meeting in May 1972 was not derailed. The Soviets successfully pressured their Indian allies not to attack Pakistan itself.

The Moscow summit meeting between Nixon and Leonid Brezhnev, the Soviet general secretary, which to Soviet chagrin followed shortly after the landmark visit of Nixon to China, focused on nuclear disarmament. According to the Nixon Doctrine, the United States only required 'sufficiency' in nuclear armaments, enabling it to inflict unacceptable damage upon the Soviet Union, as opposed to superiority or even parity in all nuclear weapons. Soviet–American nuclear arms limitation talks began in late 1969, swiftly deadlocked, but regained impetus when Kissinger's 1971 China trip convinced the Soviets to improve their own relations with the United States. Talks to reduce conventional forces in Europe began early in 1972, and at the May 1972 Moscow summit, Nixon and Brezhnev signed two treaties, jointly known as SALT-I, which took effect the following October. The ABM Treaty limited anti-ballistic missile defence sites in each country to two, neither hosting more than a hundred ABMs. The Interim Agreement froze for five years the number of nuclear warheads each side possessed, giving the Soviets numerical superiority (2,328 to the American 1,710) in exchange for accepting the American lead in multiple independent re-entry vehicles (MIRVs), the delivery system. SALT-I allowed its signatories to upgrade their nuclear weaponry provided they observed these limits.

Several Soviet–American commercial agreements followed the disarmament accords, providing for Soviet purchases of $750 million of American grain, largely financed by American credits; various business contracts; maritime understandings; and comprehensive trade agreements settling outstanding Soviet debts to the United States and promising the Soviets most-favoured-nation trading status. At a second Nixon–Brezhnev summit, held in Washington in June 1973, the two leaders signed the Agreement on the Prevention of Nuclear War, binding them to consult whenever international crises which might precipitate nuclear war between them or with other states arose, and to act 'in such a manner as to help prevent the development of situations capable of causing a dangerous exacerbation of their relations'. They also concluded four executive agreements on oceanography, transport, agricultural research, and cultural exchange, and issued a declaration of principles intended to accelerate talks at Geneva designed to produce a second, permanent nuclear arms limitation agreement (SALT-II). Airline services were expanded and trade missions established.

At a third, June 1974, summit in Moscow, the number of ABM sites permitted each superpower was reduced to one, and a Threshold Test Ban Treaty forbade underground nuclear tests exceeding 150 kilotons. At Vladivostock the following November Gerald Ford, who succeeded Nixon, and the Soviets accepted ceilings for the subsequent ten years on the numbers of missiles, single and multiple nuclear delivery vehicles, and heavy missile silos each power might possess, anticipating these would shortly be enshrined in a formal SALT-II Treaty. They expected further negotiations to extend and ideally increase these limitations beyond 1985.

The SALT agreements seemed a triumph for Nixon–Kissinger triangular diplomacy, promising further progress towards Soviet–American détente, developing Sino–American rapprochement, and the lasting relaxation of international tensions. In practice, they marked the high tide of détente. Before the Cold War began winding down in the mid-1980s, a decade of renewed Soviet–American antagonism lay ahead.

FOUR

Resurgence to Ending, 1973–1991

From the mid-1970s progress towards Soviet–American rapprochement largely halted for a decade. Within each superpower a sizeable number of influential figures deplored and sought to sabotage détente. In this period, sometimes termed the 'second Cold War', the dramatic crises of earlier decades were largely absent. Sabre-rattling and rhetoric from the American right notwithstanding, neither side displayed the overweening passionate confidence in its own ideals, principles, righteousness, and ultimate victory characteristic of the early Cold War years. Rather, a certain tired staleness, malaise, and stagnation, a near instinctive repetitive intervention in minor crises and avoidance of major confrontation, informed both Soviet and American behaviour. Each superpower faced a more challenging global situation, where former Cold War demarcating lines were often irrelevant. By the early 1970s it was ever more difficult to argue that the world was organized primarily on bipolar lines, as attention turned to north–south divisions, especially the income gap between developed and less-developed countries, and to transnational demographic, ecological, and environmental concerns which often ignored both national and Cold War boundaries.

From the early 1970s both superpowers faced major economic problems which, though they initially appeared most serious in the capitalist bloc, ultimately helped to precipitate Soviet collapse. In the United States double-digit inflation, initially triggered in part by heavy Vietnam War spending, coincided with negative real growth rates and rising unemployment, which persisted throughout the 1970s and flared up again in the early 1990s. For the first time in the twentieth century, in 1971 the balance of international trade turned and remained against the United States. As the West European and Japanese economies recovered from the Second World War, and new competitors such as South Korea and Taiwan emerged, the United States no longer enjoyed its once overwhelming post-1945 economic predominance. Symbolically, in 1971 Nixon took the American dollar, the backbone of the stability of the international financial system, off the gold standard, whose maintenance the United States now found too costly. The United States no longer had the oil reserves to keep petroleum prices low, and in the early 1970s its dependence on external oil sources became apparent. During the October 1973 Yom Kippur War oil-rich Arab states, resentful of American support for Israel, quadrupled the price of oil or withheld shipments entirely. These measures enormously strengthened the effectiveness of the existing Organization of Petroleum Exporting Countries (OPEC), which deliberately kept oil prices permanently high, fuelling American inflation. American consumers habitually used energy lavishly, making the impotence of their leaders to affect the deliberations of OPEC, several of whose members were American allies or clients, yet more galling.

Well before the 1970s, European allies of the United States had also become increasingly restive. Between 1959 and 1966 Charles de Gaulle, the independent-minded French president, withdrew his country's forces from NATO, refused to have alliance troops on French soil, and developed an independent French nuclear deterrent, thenceforth pursuing his own version of détente and *Ostpolitik*. Throughout the Vietnam War NATO allies doggedly rejected American pleas to contribute troops to the conflict. In the 1960s West Germany, virtually an American creation, ignored American suggestions to move slowly in improving relations with its Communist neighbours; in the later 1970s West German leaders refused to permit deteriorating Soviet–American relations to undercut their own détente with East Germany and the Soviet bloc.

By that time many believed Communism was making steady inroads on the West. After the 1956 Hungarian crackdown, many European Communists rejected Soviet pretensions to control the international Communist movement, especially demands that all national Communist parties allow the Soviet Union to dictate their policies. By the 1970s most West European Communist parties professed autonomy from Soviet control and readiness to respect the norms of a parliamentary system, and in several countries electoral systems facilitated governmental participation by non-majority parties. Continuing Communist strength in Italy, the revival of active Communist parties in Spain and Portugal, where Fascist rule had only just ended, and the growing appeal of the French Socialist Party and its leftwing allies, raised the spectre that NATO cabinets might include Communist representatives, a prospect which deeply alarmed American officials.

American withdrawal from Vietnam, and the subsequent northern takeover of the south two years later, effectively a humiliating American defeat, underlined the strong perception that internationally democracy was losing ground to Communism. Even so, economic difficulties mandated major American defence cuts. Between 1969 and 1975 air force squadrons declined from 169 to 110, army and marine divisions from 23 to 16, and navy combat ships from 976 to 495, limiting American ability to project its power overseas. After Vietnam the United States eschewed costly overseas military interventions. A pervasive sense of American public disarray and malaise lasted throughout the decade, intensified in 1973 and 1974 when well-publicized scandals tarnished its international reputation, forcing both Nixon and his vice-president, Spiro Agnew, to resign. On Christmas Day 1973, the veteran American diplomat David Bruce wrote: 'Except during the two Great Wars of my time, the world has never appeared in this century to be in such disarray as now. . . .

The cherished, illusory dream . . . that there would be an American Twentieth Century has been dissipated.'

Paradoxically, American disillusionment with détente developed quickly, even though the growing sense of United States international weakness might logically have been expected to encourage the moderation of Soviet–American tensions. Powerful American conservative elements, most but not all concentrated in the Republican party, distrusted what they considered the dangerous concessions détente made to the Soviets. Only four months after the 1973 Washington summit, the Soviet failure to warn the United States that Egypt, Syria, and Saudi Arabia planned a surprise attack on Israel during the Yom Kippur religious holiday undercut the consultative Soviet–American Agreement on the Prevention of Nuclear War, as did continued Soviet arms supplies to Egypt. Even more alarming, when a massive American airlift of military aid to Israel enabled the latter to launch a successful offensive against Egypt, the Soviets threatened to send troops to avert another Arab humiliation at Israeli hands. Nixon responded by publicly upgrading United States nuclear alert levels, and Brezhnev ultimately acquiesced in a cease-fire agreement and in Soviet exclusion from Kissinger's ensuing shuttle diplomacy. The Yom Kippur War implicitly cast doubt on the credibility of Soviet–American agreements to cooperate over serious international crises, providing timely ammunition for those Americans who opposed détente.

Nettled by the Vietnam War, when Congress had granted successive presidents and their advisers great latitude in devising and implementing foreign policy, American legislators sought greater independence and more influence. In 1973 Congress passed the War Powers Act, making sustained overseas deployment of United States troops contingent upon congressional approval. In August 1974 Nixon resigned, a casualty of the Watergate political scandal which from mid-1973 both preoccupied and weakened him, compromising his ability to win a SALT-II accord from the Soviets or congressional support for détente. The unelected Gerald Ford lacked the authority to challenge Congress. He personally admired Kissinger, the chief advocate of further arms negotiations, and retained him as secretary of state, but Kissinger's influence declined. Détente was closely identified with Nixon and Kissinger. Despite Kissinger's intellectual brilliance many Republican conservatives deeply distrusted him, deploring what they perceived as his pernicious and unprincipled readiness to appease, legitimize and collaborate with politically and morally unacceptable Communist regimes. Hawkish Democrats, such as Senator Henry M. Jackson of Washington, joined with them, for example in passing the Jackson–Vanik amendment of 1974. To Kissinger's fury this made the normalization of Soviet–American trade relations, promised in 1972, contingent on the lifting of Soviet restrictions on Jewish emigration, a move which led the Soviet Union to abrogate it. Throughout the 1970s Republican conservatives gained strength, peaking in 1980 when the former cinema actor Ronald Reagan, the profoundly anti-Communist governor of California, was elected president.

Well before then, détente foundered, to some degree a casualty of the unrealistically euphoric predictions of the associated benefits its supporters sometimes made. The emphasis Kissinger placed on linkage notwithstanding, it soon became clear that Soviet–American nuclear and commercial accords would not necessarily translate into Soviet moderation in other areas. The fact that after the Yom Kippur War, in which the United States threatened nuclear action, the Soviet Union was excluded from the peace process, humiliated Soviet officials. Evidence suggests that many Soviet leaders, especially military men, opposed détente, and they became increasingly influential. From the mid-1970s Soviet military expenditures and international involvements grew substantially. In 1974, at the height of détente, Russian leaders decided to develop the SS-20 medium-range nuclear missile, whose 1977 deployment against West European nations alarmed both leaders and populace in targeted countries.

Soviet nuclear parity with the United States and the novel addition of aircraft carriers to its navy encouraged influential military voices to urge direct Russian intervention in conflicts beyond Eastern Europe which they had previously avoided. With some truth, Soviet officials claimed they had never renounced their revolutionary goals or pledged to refrain from encouraging small-scale insurgencies around the world. Between 1977 and 1984 fear of ideological competition from Chinese Maoists persuaded the Soviets to upgrade such activities globally. They encouraged and even tried to create radical Marxist-

Leninist vanguard parties in Yemen and several African states. In a complicated civil war in Angola, the newly independent Portuguese colony in southern Africa, a Soviet-backed and armed faction, assisted by 11,000 Cuban troops, won power in 1976 over another political grouping the United States covertly assisted. In 1977 and 1978 Soviet and Cuban troops virtually ran the campaign when the north-east African nation Ethiopia, already a Russian client, resisted an invasion of its Ogaden province by neighbouring Somalia, to which the United States served as patron. In Zaire, the United States assumed that in the African context Angolan-based exile incursions were also Soviet-backed.

In 1978 and 1979 large-scale Soviet logistical support assisted Vietnam in its invasion of Cambodia and the subsequent Sino–Vietnamese War, and in the early 1980s Soviet military aid also benefited insurgents in the Philippines, Libya and, ending a ten-year hiatus, North Korea. Insurgent movements throughout Latin America also obtained extensive Soviet assistance, and in 1984 Soviet naval forces undertook a major Caribbean deployment.

While Soviet behaviour was apparently not a systematic drive to expand Russian influence but primarily oppor-tunistic, many Americans thought otherwise. Conserv-atives saw it as proof positive that détente had failed, and their scepticism largely undercut its further progress. Kissinger's last achievement was the Helsinki 'Final Act', the culmination of the two-year-old Conference on Security and Cooperation in Europe, which thirty-five

European states, Canada, and the United States signed in August 1975. The four-part accords covered European security, human rights, cooperation on economic, scientific, technological, and environmental matters, the free movement of individuals and ideas, and follow-up meetings to discuss enforcement, modification, and extension of the accords. All signatories recognized existing boundaries within Europe, promised to resolve disputes peacefully, to refrain from interference in the internal affairs of other signatory states, and to notify each other of large troop movements. Conservatives immediately assailed the Helsinki accords as a betrayal of Western interests which legitimized the Soviet position in Europe in exchange for meaningless human rights assurances.

In the presidential election of 1976, both left and right attacked Ford for yielding too much to the Soviets. Ironically, in practice the Helsinki accords soon became a focal rallying point for human rights advocates and anti-Soviet protestors throughout Eastern Europe. The election gave power to Jimmy Carter, a traditional liberal, whose major international preoccupation was initially to promote American values, including human rights and peaceable relations with other nations; reductions in international military spending; disarmament; and a new emphasis upon economic over defence aid. Uneasy with American overseas military deployments, Carter originally planned to withdraw United States forces from South Korea, a policy change from which State Department officials eventually dissuaded him. Initially, his administration also launched or re-energized a wide array of arms control initiatives, including a May 1977 unilateral announcement that the United States would end conventional arms transfers to Latin America and sub-Saharan Africa.

Human rights, largely disregarded throughout the Cold War, now gained new prominence. The dogged presidential focus on this issue complicated dealings by the Carter administration with both its more authoritarian allies, who resented the new insistence with which their patron stressed civil liberties, and with the Soviet Union. Well-publicized American interest in the status of prominent individual Russian dissidents, including the Nobel Prize-winning physicist Andrei Sakharov, and the Jewish dissenter Anatoly Shcharansky, infuriated the Soviets and impeded the continuing SALT-II negotiations.

Despite Carter's eagerness for a further arms control agreement, within and outside his own administration conservatives, including Zbigniew Brzezinski, his Polish-born national security adviser, as well as prominent congressmen, were deeply sceptical. Influential hawks such as Jackson sought deep reductions in the ceilings agreed in the 1975 Vladivostock accords, which they feared left the Soviets undesirably strong; sought to restrict Soviet development of long-range bombers; and suggested arms control be made contingent on a drastic reduction of Soviet activities in Africa and other developing nations. On their side the Soviets resented their continuing exclusion from the Middle East peace process even as, in a dramatic 1978 breakthrough, the

Camp David accords, Carter persuaded the Egyptian and Israeli governments to recognize each other and conclude a peace treaty. The determination Carter displayed in building a pro-Western bloc of moderate Middle Eastern states, Iran and Saudi Arabia as well as Egypt and Israel, which together received almost three-quarters of 1978 American arms shipment to the third world, undoubtedly irritated Soviet leaders.

Not until 1979 did Soviet and American officials draft a SALT-II Treaty both negotiating teams would accept, one imposing both qualitative and quantitative restrictions on American and Soviet strategic nuclear weapons and delivery systems, equalizing the ceilings on each state. Signing this treaty at Vienna in June, Carter and Brezhnev tentatively though inconclusively discussed potential agenda for a SALT-III successor. The United States Senate initially refused to ratify the treaty. Besides characterizing SALT-II as overly favourable to the Soviets, conservatives again condemned Russian activities in Africa and the presence of Soviet training brigades in Cuba. Treaty opponents also noted that the overthrow of the Shah of Iran the previous January by a radical and strongly anti-American Muslim government headed by the aged Ayatollah Khomeini had deprived the United States of intelligence posts capable of monitoring Soviet treaty compliance. Concessions by Carter, including increases in military spending and economic aid for friendly nations, close surveillance of Cuba, and establishing a permanent Caribbean military task force, proved insufficient to win them over. In practice, though, both nations observed the treaty provisions, evidence of the continuing value to both superpowers of tacit complicity in maintaining some degree of international stability.

Despite SALT-II, Soviet–Western tensions rapidly intensified. The late 1979 NATO decision to install Pershing-2 and Tomahawk tactical nuclear weapons in Western Europe, their range three to five thousand miles, to counter the Soviet SS-20s targeted on the area, alarmed the Soviets. Such weapons fell outside the scope of SALT-II, reflecting West European fears that, without their presence, the United States might not risk nuclear war on behalf of NATO allies. While this decision infuriated the Soviets, American leaders had some reason to perceive major erosions in the United States international position, as pro-Western governments fell in Iran and Nicaragua.

Since 1953 American Middle Eastern strategy had centred upon powerful, oil-rich Iran, whose abrogation of its alliance with the United States represented a major blow to American geopolitical and economic interests. The fall of the shah created serious problems, as his Islamic fundamentalist successors broke with the 'great Satan', the United States, cut off oil supplies, and in November 1979 sacked the American embassy in Teheran, holding sixty-three official American personnel hostage until Carter left office in January 1981. The hostage crisis further exacerbated American feelings of national decline and powerlessness, and a botched military rescue attempt in April 1980 underlined American humiliation. Sky-rocketing oil prices caused by an Iranian oil embargo ratcheted up inflation and again reminded American consumers how heavily their way of life depended on alien nations over whom they often had little leverage.

In Central America the July 1979 overthrow of the Nicaraguan dictator Anastasio Somoza, a long-time American ally, by a radical Marxist movement, the Sandinista Front for National Liberation, emphasized the limits of American hemispheric influence. Moderates soon left the Sandinista government as it signed a trade agreement with the Soviet Union and began to help revolutionaries in neighbouring El Salvador. A programme of covert assistance to the anti-Sandinista Nicaraguan 'Contra' rebel forces soon supplemented the economic aid packages the Carter administration and international agencies initially offered the new government.

The December 1979 Soviet intervention in Afghanistan served as the catalyst which switched United States policies to outright antagonism. In 1978 a Soviet-backed coup installed a Marxist regime in previously non-aligned Afghanistan, close to Muslim areas of Soviet territory. A growing insurgency by the Mujahedeen, an Islamic fundamentalist movement, brought Soviet military intervention to maintain the new status quo, a decision probably triggered by fears that intensifying Muslim fanaticism in Iran and Afghanistan might easily precipitate separatism within the Soviet Union. The Soviet intervention quickly became a costly war of attrition.

Carter perceived this episode, which he hyperbolically termed 'the greatest threat to peace since the Second World War', as part of a calculated Soviet strategy to gain control of the Persian Gulf and the oil-rich states surrounding it. Convinced that détente was then unattainable, he moved to reinstitute containment, embargoing Soviet purchases of American grain. He also cut drastically sales of high technology goods; announced an American boycott of the forthcoming Moscow Olympic games; and asked the Senate to postpone consideration of the SALT-II Treaty. On the defence front he demanded annual 5 per cent increases in real military spending rather than the 3 per cent he had sought since 1977; proposed American young men be compelled to register for a potential draft; and moved to create a Persian Gulf rapid deployment force. The 'Carter Doctrine' of January 1980 stated that the United States would take all necessary measures to defend the Persian Gulf. In July 1980 Carter approved the largest arms procurement programme in thirty years, while growing numbers of American missiles targeted Russian military installations.

Classic Cold War alliance strategies soon came into play. The United States moved closer to China and the military dictatorship of Pakistan, which soon became a major supply centre and sanctuary for the Afghan rebels. Aid to it, terminated after the judicial murder of its democratically elected former president, Zulfikar Ali Bhutto, was reinstated. India, the traditional enemy of Pakistan, responded by seeking Russian military aid, hosting a Brezhnev visit, and issuing a joint Russo–Indian statement condemning outside interference in south-west Asian affairs. Carter had lifted his early ban on providing arms to developing nations and by 1980 ongoing Soviet–American talks initiated in 1977 and 1978 to reduce tactical nuclear weapons and conventional forces in Europe, stalled. So, too, did talks on a comprehensive test ban treaty, a ban on anti-satellite weapons systems, demilitarization of the Indian Ocean, and the prohibition of arms transfers to third world countries.

Ronald Reagan, the fiercely anti-Communist Republican and staunch conservative who succeeded Carter in 1980, opposed all compromise with Communism and enthusiastically continued policies Carter had only reluctantly embraced. Determined to restore American pride after the to him shameful loss of domestic confidence during the 1970s, a conscious patriot who believed firmly in the American way of life, publicly convinced that American victory in the Cold War was attainable, the ever-optimistic Reagan habitually used blatantly triumphalist, anti-Soviet rhetoric, famously terming the Soviet Union an 'evil empire'. Hawkish conservatives staffed his administration.

Reagan consciously engaged the Soviets in an intensifying arms race, by which he and his advisers hoped American technological and economic superiority would strain the Soviet economy. In 1982 and 1983 the president issued directives intended to deny the Soviets Western credits, currency, trade, and technology and embargo Soviet exports of oil and natural gas to the West. A massive military buildup, boosting the defence budget from $171 billion to $376 billion between 1981 and 1986, revived several strategic nuclear weapons programmes which Carter had shelved and envisaged increasing American warships from 454 to 600, including 15 aircraft carrier groups. The number of American troops in South Korea rose by 1,600 to 37,600, while Japan, an American ally, was urged to shoulder more substantial defence commitments. In 1983 Reagan also announced that the United States would begin research on a massively expensive new ballistic-missile defence system, the Strategic Defense Initiative (SDI), popularly known as 'Star Wars', a plan to intercept and destroy all incoming nuclear missiles. If successful, this programme, which seemed likely to contravene several existing arms control treaties, would have provided the United States with substantial protection against Soviet nuclear attack, thereby destabilizing the existing *de facto* nuclear balance and quite possibly triggering a still fiercer arms race.

The Reagan administration deliberately de-emphasized human rights among its allies, consciously supporting authoritarian rulers provided they were pro-American, while assailing human rights abuses within the Soviet sphere. Covert operations intensified, as the United States offered support to anti-Communist forces around the world, providing economic aid to the dissident Polish Solidarity trade union movement, and military and economic assistance to anti-government rebels in Angola, Mujahedeen guerrillas in Afghanistan, and the anti-Sandinista Contras of Nicaragua. Efforts to overthrow the existing Nicaraguan government included CIA mining of ports and harbours. When Congress responded by passing the Boland amendment of 1984, ending all funding for Nicaraguan covert actions, the Reagan administration embroiled itself in an ill-fated secret enterprise to sell arms to Iran – thereby evading its own embargo but, officials suggested, enhancing the political standing of Iranian moderate elements – and using the proceeds to continue supplies to the Iranian contras. Revelations of these undoubtedly illegal activities and his own probable complicity in them embarrassed Reagan in his final years as president.

They did not, however, compromise Reagan's ability to reach an unprecedented new understanding with the Soviet Union. Notwithstanding his bellicose rhetoric and what sometimes seemed the near infatuation with prospective nuclear war some Reagan administration officials displayed, in practice Reagan was surprisingly pragmatic and cautious. In potentially difficult guerrilla settings, the Reagan administration habitually favoured covert operations, preferably undertaken by such surrogates as the Afghan Mujahedeen or the Nicaraguan Contras, over outright military intervention. One Vietnam War legacy was that the United States restricted the use of overt force to situations likely to produce minimum casualties. Wars were kept short and easily winnable, as in the small Caribbean island of Grenada in 1983, when in less than a week 1,900 American troops liberated the island from Marxist rule. When, almost simultaneously, radical pro-Syrian Druze Muslims bombed the Beirut barracks of an American peacekeeping force, killing 241 American soldiers, United States forces were quickly withdrawn. In 1986 suspected Libyan involvement in terrorist incidents only brought American air strikes on the Libyan capital. Alarmed that the lengthy war Iran and

Iraq began in 1980 threatened Persian Gulf sea lanes carrying international oil supplies, the Reagan administration chose the deterrent but noncommittal course of deploying American naval forces to the area.

Despite campaign pledges, Reagan likewise neither derecognized the mainland nor restored American relations with Taiwan. In 1982 the Reagan administration reached an understanding with China on Taiwan, after which the Chinese gave some support to the Afghan Mujahedeen rebels, Sino–American trade increased, and Reagan made a 1984 state visit to Beijing. By 1984 domestic political considerations suggested that the president moderate his anti-Soviet line. He faced a re-election campaign against a liberal opponent just as his American and European nuclear build-up, and the stalemating of inconclusive arms control talks begun in 1981, had generated substantial public support in both America and Europe for a nuclear freeze. In September 1984 Reagan proposed combining all major ongoing nuclear weapons talks into one package, and Soviet leaders soon agreed to participate.

Reagan's mellowing coincided with the culmination of evolving Soviet problems dating back at least to the late 1970s, when all major Soviet economic indicators suddenly declined. The economic growth rate, 5.2 per cent from 1966 to 1970, fell to 2.7 per cent, and growth in industrial production, investment, productivity, and consumption also dropped, sometimes to negative or near-negative levels. Oil production levelled off, and from 1979 to 1982 Russia suffered droughts and poor harvests. Lagging modernization in such old industries as steel, combined with the tardy introduction of new technology, such as computers, left the Soviet Union trailing the West. The nature of Soviet economy and society discouraged individualist inventors and entrepreneurs whose efforts contributed to Western economic growth. From the early 1970s Soviet living standards, health care, and life expectancy all dropped while infant mortality rose. When such problems appeared, serious systemic flaws in the Soviet command economy, including its autarkic nature and the consequent absence of independent institutions which could provide credit and capital, plus the non-existence of fiscal economic incentives, conspired to facilitate collapse rather than reform.

Empire imposed added burdens. By the mid-1980s Soviet military spending absorbed 13–14 per cent (18 per cent according to some figures) of Gross National Product, as opposed to 10–12 per cent in the early 1960s, diverting funds from domestic economic development. Most countries in Eastern Europe, the core of Soviet security concerns, still resented Soviet domination. The growing Polish Solidarity labour movement of the late 1970s was only the newest of successive East European challenges to Soviet rule. In Poland the economic difficulties all Europe experienced during the 1970s contributed to the rise of Solidarity. Western powers showed their usual caution when Poland introduced military rule in 1981, offering only the standard moral support and rhetorical condemnation. Even so, within Poland the continuing covert strength of Solidarity undercut Soviet hegemonic legitimacy. Instead of winning popularity by offering additional assistance, in

1982 the Soviets cut by 10 per cent oil shipments to Eastern European allies, whose own economies also suffered from rigid autarky. Globally assertive Soviet foreign policies carried a high price tag, as Soviet clients throughout the world demonstrated insatiable appetites for economic and military aid, while expanding Russian overseas activities almost automatically triggered determined American responses in opposition, which in turn demanded further Soviet expenditures. The lengthy Afghan intervention, which lasted until 1989, embroiled Soviet troops in a costly and unwinnable guerrilla war producing heavy casualties, an expensive and demoralizing entanglement which echoed American involvement in Vietnam.

Until 1985, when the young and energetic Mikhail Gorbachev became Communist Party general secretary, successive elderly and ailing Soviet leaders did little to address these problems. Gorbachev, though a committed Communist, was of a generation which laid far greater emphasis upon freedom of thought and choice. Initially he hoped to reform the Soviet economy and society from within, strengthening Communism through the twin policies of *perestroika* (economic reform) and *glasnost* (openness), but the heavy budgetary burdens of Soviet military and foreign policy impeded this strategy. Moreover, the enormously costly SDI programme Reagan had recently proposed was likely to demand massive additional Soviet military spending. Admirers of Reagan have suggested that, fully aware of Soviet economic fragility, he instituted the early 1980s defence build-up as a conscious strategy to engineer the collapse of the Soviet empire. This theory seems to ascribe overmuch prescience to the president, none of whose advisers or intelligence staff predicted the Soviet Union's dissolution, and most of whom characterized it as a formidable foe. Emphasizing the American contribution above all else ignores also the impact of deepseated internal Soviet weaknesses and other contributory factors. It seems likely, however, that the Reagan arms buildup and its prospective continuation imposed appreciable additional strains on the increasingly compromised Soviet economy, impelling Gorbachev to seek a new rapprochement with the West.

Once progress began, it was rapid, in part because the domestic reforms Gorbachev instituted tended further to weaken his country. American and European leaders were initially wary of responding to Gorbachev's overtures, suspecting these were only empty gestures designed to persuade the West to relax its guard. In Europe, where since the late 1970s the collapse of détente and the subsequent nuclear buildup had provoked public alarm and a determination to preserve the pan-European gains of the previous two decades, Gorbachev quickly won great popularity. Margaret Thatcher, the hard-line British prime minister whom Reagan found a political soulmate, urged her colleague to work with the Soviet leader, while Reagan – perhaps because, as a former movie star, he tended to believe in sudden happy endings – was far readier than many of his advisers to trust Gorbachev. Domestic economic factors may also have impelled Reagan towards rapprochement. Deep tax cuts meant that heavy government budget deficits financed the 1980s defence buildup, and in November 1987 an unexpected Wall Street stock-market crash suggested American economic fundamentals might be undesirably weak.

In that year the superpowers signed the Intermediate Nuclear Forces Treaty, eliminating all medium-range missiles in Europe, and imposing strong verification procedures. The Strategic Arms Reduction Treaty (START-I) Treaty, which Gorbachev and George Bush, who succeeded Reagan, concluded in 1991, cut long-range weapons dramatically, though after the dissolution of the Soviet Union the failure of Ukraine and Belarus to ratify it and the lack of Soviet funds for dismantling weapons scheduled for destruction made its implementation slow and patchy. Further START reductions followed in 1993.

Gorbachev himself intended to strengthen, not destroy, both the Soviet Union and the Soviet empire, but events quickly gained their own momentum and overtook him. *Glasnost*-inspired criticism on occasion undercut the economic restructuring of *perestroika* and, if anything, reforms initially intensified existing economic problems. Reluctant to inflict the pain incumbent on full-scale economic restructuring, Gorbachev opted for half-measures, retaining much of the command economy structure of price supports and controls, which undercut those reforms he initiated. Inflation, shortages, strikes, and falling productivity resulted. Increasingly, budgetary difficulties led Gorbachev to dismantle expensive Soviet military commitments whether or not the West offered matching concessions.

In 1985 Gorbachev extended *glasnost* and *perestroika* to Soviet satellites in Eastern Europe, hoping thereby to strengthen Communism in those countries, but in practice promoting rapidly accelerating East European criticism of Communism. Although the Soviet hold on this once vital and unnegotiable security interest was increasingly precarious, in 1988 Gorbachev unilaterally reduced the Soviet armed forces by 500,000 and withdrew 10,000 tanks, 8,500 artillery systems, and 800 combat units from Eastern Europe. The Soviet Politburo decided against intervention should these satellites choose to reject Communism, institute free elections, and leave the Soviet empire, which by 1990 all had done. Symbolically, in 1989 the Berlin Wall was dismantled, and the following year the two Germanies united, retaining NATO membership despite Soviet objections. These humiliating blows to Soviet prestige and the inability of Communism to retain popular support outside the Soviet Union cast doubt on all the supposed achievements of their system since 1945. Responding to the new situation, in November 1991 NATO changed its military doctrine to reflect the reality that an attack across the East German border was no longer likely.

Between 1989 and 1991 the Soviet Union also liquidated its expensive global commitments to revolutionary and quasi-revolutionary regimes and other clients in Nicaragua, Afghanistan, El Salvador, Ethiopia, Cuba, Vietnam, and elsewhere. A new rapprochement with China mirrored the warming of Soviet–Western relations and made it unnecessary to maintain large Soviet forces on the Sino–Soviet border. Only in the Soviet Union proper and the Baltic republics of Lithuania, Latvia, and Estonia, forcibly incorporated into the Soviet Union in

1940, did Gorbachev attempt to combat separatism with military coercion, behaviour which Western powers, anxious to maintain him in power, tolerated, although the insistent Baltic republics eventually regained independence in 1991. Until the late 1980s Gorbachev sought to reserve for the Communist Party a special status in Soviet politics, but attempts by party officials to sabotage his policies led him to reduce their privileges, and in March 1990 he abolished Article 6 of the Soviet Constitution, which had guaranteed the Communist Party a 'leading role' in government.

Alarmed by the prevailing Soviet economic anarchy, Western leaders and institutions were slow to provide substantial loans and credits. Their preoccupation with the expensive Gulf War of January 1991, when a NATO coalition reversed the August 1990 takeover by Iraq of oil-rich Kuwait, a Western ally, left little attention or aid for Russia. As his Western reputation grew, Gorbachev's domestic popularity plummeted. In August 1991 a military coup almost overthrew him, but popular resistance led by Boris Yeltsin, the independent-minded new president of the Russian republic, reinstated him as Soviet president. Hoping to sustain Gorbachev in power, later that year the United States extended further grain credits to the Soviet Union, though a recession made it impossible to win congressional support for the major aid package Gorbachev sought. Shortly afterwards the Soviet Union itself dissolved, replaced by a short-lived Commonwealth of Independent States, of which Yeltsin was elected the first president.

Conclusion

On 12 November 1990 the Conference on Security and Cooperation in Europe formally announced the end of the Cold War. This did not mark the demise of Communism. Cold War antagonisms still inform the Asian strategic picture, both the pattern of alliance relationships and the current divisions between North and South Korea and China and Taiwan reflecting their impact on the Pacific region. Yet, despite some efforts to portray China as the next great United States enemy, these are now subsumed in a pattern of complicated intra-regional relationships, in which a weakened and often resentful Russia participates, rather than viewed within the framework of a global struggle for ideological, strategic, and economic dominance. The Cold War began with a Soviet–Western confrontation in Europe. Once it collapsed in that region, it was widely felt to have ended.

Although much historical and literary writing treated the two major opponents as mirror images of each other, certain asymmetries existed between them. In the 1950s and 1960s, at the height of the Cold War, the United States alliance network was decidedly more systematic and wide-ranging than the Soviet, whose core always remained Eastern Europe. This perhaps reflected the degree to which American post-1945 economic and strategic interests were far more genuinely global than those of the Soviet Union, and the much broader extent of its informal empire. On both sides, however, the input of allies and clients was often important in shaping the Cold War in any given area. On occasion, as with Taiwan, both Koreas, and both Vietnamese regimes, Cold War preoccupations also offered relatively weak states the opportunity to manipulate far mightier patrons.

The rapid implosion of the Soviet Union in the 1980s might suggest that it was, to quote Mao Zedong, only a 'paper tiger'. John Lewis Gaddis has argued recently with hindsight that from the early 1960s onwards Soviet possession of nuclear weapons masked Russian economic weakness, which should have denied it genuine great-power status. Even so, until the 1980s the Soviet Union succeeded in maintaining a formidable military profile, which could not be discounted and which enabled it to project its power and protect its perceived interests in Eastern Europe and elsewhere. In *The Fifty Years War* (1995) Richard Crockatt suggests that the ultimate Cold War vindication of the United States stemmed from the degree to which American power, unlike its Soviet equiv-alent, was firmly based upon both economic and military strength and on American ability to tap the resources of the world capitalist system to promote its military objectives.

Cultural influence, prestige, and power were important in the Cold War. Geir Lundestad has suggested that the American sphere of influence, unlike the Soviet, con-stituted an 'empire by invitation', one of its major strengths the fact that American clients and allies accepted or even sought that status willingly, to gain perceived benefits such as military security and economic aid. A cynic might justifiably question how accurately this description depicted the reality of the relationship between the United States and other powers in Latin America, Africa, and much of Asia. In these areas the majority of the multi-lateral defence pacts the United States initiated fizzled out or were deliberately abrogated. The Lundestad thesis is more convincing when related to American dealings with Western Europe and Australasia, and perhaps with some of its Asian allies, particularly Japan. Here, where American policy was most successful, allies and client states forcefully urged the United States to assist them and enter into defence commitments to protect them from perceived enemies or threats.

When France expelled NATO forces in the 1960s, American officials refrained from attempts to coerce their ally to reverse its decision; when East European nations rebelled against Soviet domination, Russian tanks compelled them to reconsider. Reliance on repression won the Soviets fundamentally unreliable allies. American methods were clearly more effective. East European nations, after forty-five years of Soviet predominance and more than three decades in the Warsaw Pact, sought to end their Soviet associations immediately the opportunity offered, and often to join NATO. West European nations, by contrast, fearful that the changed international bal-ance of forces might lead the United States to abandon NATO, regarded the organization as a stabilizing force and sought new functions to justify its continuing existence. Despite Communist claims to represent the morally superior ideology, the overwhelming majority of refugees fled from the Communist to the non-Communist world. In terms of 'soft power', the degree to which the perceived cultural, moral, and intellectual values of one nation attract others, the United States clearly enjoyed the advantage.

This should not obscure how severely, even in the West, Cold War priorities distorted public discourse and free press operations. Within Communist countries controlled media and routine state repression of dissent of all kinds stifled public opposition to Cold War policies. Western methods were more subtle, but still detrimental, reflecting established close ties between governments and the most influential organs of opinion. At least until the Vietnam War most of the Western press, particularly quality journals, accepted and validated the official line near uncritically, albeit with caveats over McCarthyist excesses. The mass circulation popular press was seldom in doubt. In the early Cold War Western media characterization of Communism as a leftist variety of Fascism effectively endorsed international intervention and domestic governmental repression.

Restrictions on Western public opinion should not, however, be exaggerated. Despite pervasive media identification with Cold War policies and the efforts of Western security services, a strong transatlantic nuclear disarmament movement emerged in the 1950s and 1960s, reviving dramatically in the 1980s. Massive popular protests against the Vietnam War drastically reduced the readiness of European governments to assist the United States in south-east Asia, while undercutting American determination to continue its intervention. Likewise, notwithstanding the fears President Eisenhower expressed that there existed an American 'military-industrial complex' with vested interests in high defence budgets and the perpetuation of Cold War antagonisms, as Soviet–Western tensions relaxed in the 1980s, military spending declined precipitately.

Looking back on the Cold War, it is hard not to conclude, as some historians have done, that 'we all lost the Cold War', in the sense that in most cases the resources devoted to it could have served better and far more productive purposes. The Cold War gave an object lesson in how, once an international antagonism is established, it acquires a self-propelling momentum. Nuclear weapons and the understandable fears political leaders displayed of the consequences of outright conflict enforced a discipline of terror, so that in practice each Cold War antagonist exhibited considerable caution in dealing with the other, hesitating to trespass too far on the interests of its rival. Yet on both sides mutual distrust was so firmly entrenched as to render elusive success in the recurrent efforts towards compromise, coexistence, and understanding. This led it to become a virtual contest of attrition, ending only when the costs to one principal actor rose so high that its burdens became unsustainable.

Further Reading

This essay gives a mere sampling of the voluminous and ever growing literature on the Cold War. For more detailed guidance readers should consult such major reference guides as Thomas S. Arms, *Encyclopedia of the Cold War* (New York: Facts on File, 1994); Benjamin Frankel, ed., *The Cold War, 1945–1991*, 3 vols. (Detroit: Gale Research, 1992); and Thomas Parrish, *The Cold War Encyclopedia* (New York: Holt, 1996). The newest scholarship on the Cold War often appears initially in journals, including: the *Bulletin* and *Working Papers* of the Cold War International History Project (CWIHP); *Diplomatic History*; *Diplomacy and Statecraft*; the *International History Review*; and the *Journal of Cold War History*.

Archival sources on the Cold War are enormous and constantly growing, increasingly from Communist bloc countries as well as the Western powers. Many of the most recent such materials appear in the CWIHP *Bulletin* and its associated website, http://www.seas.gwu.edu/nsarchive/cwihp. Multi-volume published documentary series include the indispensable *Foreign Relations of the United States* (Washington: Government Printing Office); and the less extensive *Documents on British Policy Overseas* (London: Her Majesty's Stationery Office).

Useful syntheses include: S.J. Ball, *The Cold War: An International History 1947–1991* (London: Arnold, 1998); Richard Crockatt, *The Fifty Years War: The United States and the Soviet Union in World Politics, 1941–1991* (London: Routledge, 1995); David S. Painter, *The Cold War: An Interdisciplinary History* (New York: Routledge, 1999); David Reynolds, *One World Divisible: A Global History Since 1945* (New York: Norton, 1999); and Martin Walker, *The Cold War: A History* (New York: Henry Holt, 1994).

Broad surveys of post-1945 United States foreign policies are: Warren I. Cohen, *The Cambridge History of American Foreign Relations*: Volume IV, *America in the Age of Soviet Power, 1945–1991* (Cambridge: Cambridge University Press, 1993); Thomas G. Paterson, *Meeting the Communist Threat: Truman to Reagan* (New York: Oxford University Press, 1994); Michael S. Sherry, *In the Shadow of War: The United States Since the 1930s* (New Haven: Yale University Press, 1995); and Donald W. White, *The American Century: The Rise and Decline of the United States as a World Power* (New Haven: Yale University Press, 1996). Two instructive works by Ernest R. May are *'Lessons' of the Past: The Use and Misuse of History in American Foreign Policy* (New York: Oxford University Press, 1973); and *American Cold War Strategy: Interpreting NSC 68* (Boston: St Martin's Press, 1993). An interesting non-American view is Geir Lundestad, *The American 'Empire' and Other Studies of US Foreign Policy in a Comparative Perspective* (New York: Oxford University Press, 1990).

An unrivalled synthesis of recent scholarship and evidence on the early Cold War is John Lewis Gaddis, *We Now Know: Rethinking Cold War History* (New York: Oxford University Press, 1997). The national security interpretation of Cold War origins is most fully presented in Melvyn P. Leffler, *A Preponderance of Power: National Security, the Truman Administration, and the Cold War* (Stanford: Stanford University Press, 1992); and Michael J. Hogan, *A Cross of Iron: Harry S. Truman and the Origins of the National Security State 1945–1954* (Cambridge: Cambridge University Press, 1998). A stimulating Russian perspective drawing heavily on Soviet archives is Vladislav Zubok and Constantine Pleshakov, *Inside the Kremlin's Cold War: From Stalin to Khrushchev* (Cambridge, MA: Harvard University Press, 1996). Varying assessments of the Marshall Plan are: Michael J. Hogan, *The Marshall Plan: America, Britain, and the Reconstruction of Western Europe, 1947–1952* (Cambridge: Cambridge University Press, 1987); and Alan Milward, *The Reconstruction of Western Europe, 1945–51* (Berkeley: University of California Press, 1984). Examples of recent scholarship on Britain's precipitating role in the Cold War include: Alan Bullock,

Ernest Bevin: Foreign Secretary, 1945–1951 (New York: Norton, 1993); Anne Deighton, *The Impossible Peace: Britain, the Division of Germany, and the Origins of the Cold War* (New York: Oxford University Press, 1990); and Randall Bennett Woods, *A Changing of the Guard: Anglo-American Relations, 1941–1946* (Chapel Hill: University of North Carolina Press, 1990).

Various aspects of the Cold War beyond Europe are covered in: Walter LaFeber, *The Clash: U.S.–Japanese Relations Throughout History* (New York: Norton, 1997); Bruce Cumings, *The Origins of the Korean War*, 2 vols (Princeton: Princeton University Press, 1981–1990); William Stueck, *The Korean War: An International History* (Princeton: Princeton University Press, 1995); Rosemary Foot, *The Practice of Power: U.S. Relations with China since 1949* (Oxford: Clarendon, 1995); George C. Herring, *America's Longest War: The United States and Vietnam, 1950–1975*, 3rd edn (New York: McGraw-Hill, 1996); R. B. Smith, *An International History of the Vietnam War*, 3 vols (London: Macmillan, 1983–); H. W. Brands, *The Specter of Neutralism: The United States and the Emergence of the Third World, 1947–1960* (New York: Columbia University Press, 1989); Gabriel Kolko, *Confronting the Third World: United States Foreign Policy, 1945–1980* (New York: Pantheon, 1988); and Bruce Robellet Kuniholm, *The Origins of the Cold War in the Near East: Great Power Diplomacy in Iran, Turkey, and Greece* (Princeton: Princeton University Press, 1980).

Among the multifarious works on the Cuban missile crisis are: James Blight, Bruce Allyn and David Welch, eds, *Cuba on the Brink: Castro, the Missile Crisis and the Soviet Collapse* (New York: Pantheon, 1993); Blight and Welch, eds, *Intelligence and the Cuban Missile Crisis* (London: Frank Cass, 1998); Dino A. Brugioni, *Eyeball to Eyeball: The Inside Story of the Cuban Missile Crisis* (New York: Random House, 1991); Aleksandr Fursenko and Timothy Naftali, *One Hell of a Gamble: Khrushchev, Castro, and Kennedy, 1958–1964* (New York: Norton, 1997); and Ernest R. May and Philip D. Zelikow, eds, *The Kennedy Tapes: Inside the White House during the Cuban Missile Crisis* (Cambridge: Harvard University Press, 1997).

The extensive literature on Nixon and Kissinger includes: Stephen E. Ambrose, *Nixon*, 3 vols (New York: Simon and Schuster, 1987–1991); Willliam Burr, ed., *The Kissinger Transcripts: The Top-Secret Talks with Beijing & Moscow* (New York: The New Press, 1998); Joan Hoff, *Nixon Reconsidered* (New York: Norton, 1994); and Walter Isaacson, *Kissinger: A Biography* (New York: Simon and Schuster, 1992). Détente and its aftermath are thoroughly covered in: Raymond Garthoff, *Détente and Confrontation: American–Soviet Relations from Nixon to Reagan*, rev. edn (Washington: Brookings Institution, 1994); *The Great Transition: American–Soviet Relations and the End of the Cold War* (Washington: Brookings Institution, 1994); Robert Litwak, *Détente and the Nixon Doctrine: American Foreign Policy and the Pursuit of Stability, 1969–1976* (New York: Cambridge University Press, 1984); Gaddis Smith, *Morality, Reason and Power: American Diplomacy in the Carter Years* (New York: Hill and Wang, 1986); Michael Beschloss and Strobe Talbott, *At the Highest Levels: The Inside Story of the End of the Cold War* (London: Little Brown, 1993); David Pryce-Jones, *The War That Never Was: The Fall of the Soviet Empire, 1885–1991* (London: Weidenfeld and Nicolson, 1995); and Richard Ned Lebow and Janice Gross Stein, *We All Lost the Cold War* (Princeton: Princeton University Press, 1994).

Among the more enlightening Cold War memoirs are: Dean Acheson, *Present at the Creation: My Years in the State Department* (New York: Norton, 1969); George F. Kennan, *Memoirs 1925–1950* (Boston: Atlantic Little Brown, 1967); Richard M. Nixon, *RN: The Memoirs of Richard Nixon* (New York: Warner Books, 1978); Henry Kissinger, *White House Years* (Boston: Little Brown, 1979); *Years of Upheaval* (Boston: Little Brown, 1982); *Years of Renewal* (New York: Simon and Schuster, 1999); Vyaschlev Molotov, *Molotov Remembers: Inside Kremlin Politics: Conversations with Felix Chuev*, ed. Albert Resis (Chicago: Ivan R. Dee, 1993); Nikita Khrushchev, *Khrushchev Remembers: The Glasnost Tapes*, ed. Jerrold Schechter (Boston: Little Brown, 1990); and Andrei Gromyko, *Memoirs* (New York: Doubleday, 1989).

Index

INDEX

INDEX

INDEX